THE
PARADISE
PARADIGM

On Creating a World of Compassion, Freedom, and Prosperity

By G. D. ALLPORT

 E. DIANNE PUBLISHING

Cover and Interior design by Lightbourne, Inc., www. Lightbourne.com

Library of Congress Cataloging-in-Publication data

Allport, Glen Davies
    The Paradise Paradigm: On creating a world of compassion, freedom, and prosperity / G. D. Allport—1st ed., revised

Includes an index

ISBN 0-9746275-1-8 First edition

ISBN-10: 0-9746275-2-6 First edition, revised
ISBN-13: 978-0-9746275-2-6 First edition, revised

1. Social change 2. Social psychology

10 9 8 7 6 5 4 3 2 1

First edition, revised.

Printed in the United States of America

To a world that *could* be—and which
slumbers within us all, waiting.

CONTENTS

———— • ————

Preface 1
Introduction 7

SECTION ONE: The Idea of Paradise

CHAPTER 1: The Hunger for a Compassionate World 13
If love can save the world, why hasn't it?

CHAPTER 2: Paradigms: Tools of Perception 19
Non-coercive, decentralized, powerful, appropriate

CHAPTER 3: The Paradise Paradigm 29
*"Raising enough emotionally healthy children will
create a healthy world"*

CHAPTER 4: The New World 45
*Another example of sweeping change from a
paradigm shift*

SECTION TWO: Understanding Paradise

CHAPTER 5: Sensitive Dependence on Early Conditions 53
*Early experience affects character, behavior,
and health*

CHAPTER 6: Love and Freedom 63
The Fundamentals of Paradise

CHAPTER 7: The Human Condition Dramatized 83
If fiction is "symbolic," the question arises: of what?

CHAPTER 8: Prevention Is the Only Long-term Solution 91
*We cannot cure the emotional damage of
several billion adults, but we can start
reducing trauma to children*

CHAPTER 9: What Is Love? 97
A topic that should need no discussion—but does

SECTION THREE: The Road to Paradise

CHAPTER 10: Positive Action 115
An invitation

CHAPTER 11: Obstacles and Dangers 125
*Even the dangers of technology are, at bottom,
mostly problems of emotional damage and coercion*

CHAPTER 12: The Benefits of Compassion and Freedom 133
We will see them long before the job is finished

Appendices

1. Further Reading 143

2. "Love One Another" 151

3. Primal Theory 157

4. 17,421 Examples of "Sensitive Dependence on
   Early Conditions": An introduction to *Turning
   gold into lead*, by Vincent J. Felitti, MD 161

Acknowledgments 173

Notes 177

Index 185

PREFACE

———— • ————

THE PARADISE PARADIGM was written to spread the idea that a better world is possible, to provide a glimpse of that world and a conceptual framework for understanding it, and to encourage readers to adopt the framework and to share it with others. Ultimately, the goal is to change the world for the better, widely and dramatically.

This "better world" is one you already know, because it is the world of your heart. It is the world you *expected* to find when you arrived on this earth. Regardless of your race, religion, or nationality, you were born for a world of love and compassion. You were born for a world without war, genocide, or other human cruelty. You were born for a world of reasonable abundance—not of neurotic over-supply and greed, but a world where the basics of life are met, reliably and without trauma.

You needed and expected such a world at birth because nature designed you for that world and for no other.

Our primary needs, strengths, and desires are clearly best suited to an environment of compassion, freedom, and prosperity. A moment's reflection will confirm this: such a world is the one in which you would feel most at home. It is the world that would bring out your best, especially had you lived in it from the start. A free, compassionate, and prosperous world would be the safest and healthiest world for your children. It would be the best environment for your neighbors and friends.

1

Is such a world really possible?

Oh, yes: such a world *is* possible, without question. Indeed, *preventing* it from coming into being takes real work. Small portions of this world, and partial implementations of it, are available for all to see. However, most of us do not see these glimmers of Paradise and often we do not understand their importance when we *do* see them. But these micro examples and partial implementations of Paradise do exist, and we will discuss their significance later in this book.

It is an important point that this Paradise—this "better world"—is no supernatural daydream or unworkable, neurotic, coercive utopia. The free, compassionate, and prosperous society we seek is *real* and it is here, now, in this world, for a fortunate few already. Not only is it practical and realistic: it is far *more* practical and realistic than the systems we endure today.

In the near future, technology will be powerful enough that a healthy, real Paradise may be the *only* world in which we can survive.

– 2 –

NONE OF THE MATERIAL in this book is complicated or difficult to grasp. My goal is certainly audacious, but it is also simple and straightforward. In any case, we are all human beings and each of us has the equipment to understand the human condition.

That is good, because "experts" are famous for being at odds on human issues. Even those inclined to accept expert opinion uncritically must make their own decisions in this area, if only to choose among the various schools of thought. At any rate, I have no more authority here than you do: I am a human being and am interested in the human condition.

The questions I would ask before you begin are these:

❍ Are you happy with the *human* world as it is? Not only in your home or neighborhood, but in the world at large?
❍ If not, what would make it better?

⊙ And finally: how important is this topic?

Those questions, along with my own longing for a healthier, saner, and more compassionate world, led to the book you hold in your hands.

Because feelings are the key element here, it is important to take enough time with the material to open up to it. The concepts are not complicated, but they do push against our emotional defenses. To get the most out of this book, give it time to percolate down, to settle in, to become a part of your inner landscape.

– 3 –

REAL CHANGE will require perceptual shifts of great magnitude.

The approaches we have tried for creating a better world—and in particular for ending evil via politics, religion, education, etc.— have failed, utterly, despite all the hard work, despite the earnest activism, despite genuinely good intentions, despite the many small victories, and despite the astonishing success we have had in areas such as technology. The world is still run nearly everywhere by tyrants (elected or otherwise), hundreds of millions are starving needlessly, torture and other atrocity is commonplace in many nations, genocide and war are in the news frequently, people are miserable enough to use drugs (legal and otherwise) by the train-load in nations around the world, and the sorry list of such symptoms is nearly endless.

Prediction: Traditional efforts to end evil, misery, and tyranny in this world will continue to fail. They will fail because they do not take fundamentals sufficiently into account. They will fail because they are based upon perceptions of reality that are largely inaccurate.

If we are to succeed, we must replace old paradigms with new and more accurate paradigms. That change of view will make this book seem jarring at times, and I hope you will allow the framework to take shape in your mind. It may help to know that the book's message is neither "liberal" nor "conservative." It won't matter whether you are Christian, atheist, Buddhist, Muslim, Hindu, or any other religion. The guiding star for this book is simply that a healthier world is both possible and necessary, and that we must actively create that world if it is ever to exist.

– 4 –

I AM CERTAINLY NOT ASKING you to take what I say uncritically; I ask instead that you think for yourself, and decide whether the ideas here make sense to you. That will be easy to do because we are talking more about *preferences* than about science. Science can tell us what happens in response to one approach or another, but it cannot tell us *what we prefer.*

Love or hate? Compassion or cruelty? Freedom or tyranny? These are issues of the heart, not of science. They are issues of preference, in other words. Throughout history, societies have differed in their dominant preferences. In ancient Greece, for example, Athens was democratic, literate, and artistic, while Sparta was austere, authoritarian, and militaristic. Human character and behavior were channeled in the direction of the locally dominant preferences. In turn, these two societies mirrored the preferences of their inhabitants. Living in Athens was a very different experience than living in Sparta; in Sparta, regimentation, obedience to authority, and stoic acceptance of pain and hardship were not merely ideals: they were common features of everyday life.

If science cannot tell us *what* we prefer, it *can* tell us how to move things in the direction we *do* prefer. If we want a world where people feel more connected to each other and show more compassion than is typical today, then science—along with simple observation—tells us that we need to increase the number of infants and children who are treated warmly, lovingly, and compassionately as they grow up. If we'd prefer more adults who are unconnected, violent, and cold—hearted or insensitive, then science can tell us how to bring about *that.* The same is true for other preferences we might have for society.

There is a tremendous amount of material to support the book's thesis—in these pages, at the website (*http://www.paradise-paradigm.net*), and in your daily newspaper, as well as in scientific and medical journals. Entire books have been written, for example, about the importance of early experience in creating the tone and character of later life; some are quoted in this book and several are listed in the "Further Reading" section.

But you won't need any of that, I suspect. You've seen the material, or enough of it, already. The purpose of this book is not so much to provide *new* information as to put the information you already *have* into a particular framework.

That framework is the message of this book. I offer it as sincerely as I know how, in hopes that you will consider it with an open mind and an open heart.

March 14, 2006

INTRODUCTION

———— • ————

How This Book Came to Be Written

MORE THAN THIRTY YEARS AGO, I attended a university seminar which presented the results of a psychology experiment.

Psychology was certainly in need of breakthroughs. "It's a sick world," as the saying has it, and psychologists have always agreed. Early in the twentieth century, for example, Freud published a book titled The Psychopathology of Everyday Life. Decades later, another famous psychologist (Wilhelm Reich, who had been a student of Freud's) coined the phrase "emotional plague" to describe what he saw as the human condition.

History backs up their opinions with a vengeance; so do current events. As this is written—decades after they wrote, and more than a century after Freud published his landmark The Interpretation of Dreams in 1900—any newspaper validates their dark views on the human condition, if not their theories of how and why it came to be in such a state.

– 2 –

AT THE TIME OF THE SEMINAR, American military involvement in Vietnam was at its peak. Much of the world was in turmoil; the Soviet Union, Red China, and other repressive governments were torturing, murdering, and unjustly imprisoning huge numbers of their own people. The stage was being set for Pol Pot and his

Khmer Rouge to create "the killing fields" in Cambodia, and of course many other governments were doing equally horrible things to their citizens, although usually on a smaller scale.

At the same time, hundreds of thousands were dying each year from tobacco and alcohol—by liver disease, lung cancer, drunk-driving accidents, and by other problems caused from smoke or drink. Other drugs were in wide use as well; some legal, some not.

Theft, murder, assault, and other crime was in the news, daily.

Clearly, Reich's "emotional plague" had not abated.

– 3 –

HERE, IN SUCH A WORLD, was the experiment that psychologists, therapists, and students of psychology had come to hear about, and which others in the field had believed important enough to con- ceive and carry out:

> It had long been known that human or animal subjects would quickly associate one stimulus with another that immediately follows. The researchers had asked volunteers to press a button when a light came on in a panel in front of them; shortly before the light came on, a barely audible noise was sounded. Subjects were not told about the noise.
>
> Inevitably, subjects began responding to the sound, not the light. By the time they pressed the button, or perhaps a heartbeat later, the light had come on, so it may be (not that it matters for our purpose today) that they were unaware they were responding to a sound instead of to the light.
>
> The source of the noise was moved, in five degree incre- ments, from the front to the side of the subjects. Measurements were taken to see if this change in position affected the response time.
>
> It did not.

– 4 –

THAT WAS THE END of the experiment, but not of my reaction to it.

A powerful sense of distress came over me as the presentation wore on. The speaker took an hour or more describing the experiment, which in turn had taken weeks or months to set up and perform. After data had been collected, time had been spent analyzing it, writing a paper about the data, digging out references to related experiments, discussing the data with team members, and polishing the writing before presenting the paper to the world.

During all this time, remember, much of that world had been starving, at war, or living in fear of its own government. Murder, theft, fraud, assault, and other crime had been in the news constantly. Around the globe, people had been drowning their sorrows and dulling their pain with drugs of every kind.

Yet here is what the researchers—in the field of human nature and human behavior specifically—had spent their time and efforts on: moving the source of a sound, in five degree increments, to see if this change would have an effect on people's response times.

What, as they say, is wrong with this picture?

– 5 –

THAT NIGHT I had a vivid dream: the seminar was again in progress, but this time smoke gradually began curling upward from behind a table. Flames soon appeared, small and feeble at first but then spreading. Wallpaper crackled and blackened as the fire devoured it; acrid smoke wafted from melting plastic seat cushions on the stackable metal chairs; drapery rustled as the air began to stir from the heat.

Oddly, the researchers and attendees became figures from the Victorian age, with formal starched collars and other archaic dress. Even their movements and facial expressions became subtly different. They began to move around the room, examining it, studying details carefully and scientifically.

They completely ignored the fire.

Instead, they measured the hinges on the doors, carefully jotting down figures in notebooks and discussing the significance of what had been found. The researchers inspected the nap of the carpet, the indentations made by chair legs, and the patterns of wear. They emptied wastebaskets and inventoried the contents. Moving on in small groups, they turned their attention to other detail elements in the room. They were always excited, in muted Victorian fashion, by what they found. Intelligent-sounding discussions could be heard, as learned professionals and bright students alike sought to understand the meaning of it all, to convey that meaning to others, and, of course, to appear wiser and more profound than anyone else in the room.

Meanwhile, the air began to shimmer from the heat, as the flames grew.

– 6 –

NOT LONG AFTERWARD, I left the university, never to return. Eventually—no longer so young—I decided to write about what I had wanted, with all my heart, on the day of that seminar. It was what I had wanted every *other* day of my life, as well.

What I wanted, then and now, was simple: a world without human evil—or at least a world without so very *much* evil. This world would also have less misery and more compassion. In *this* world, psychopathology would not be the default condition of people everywhere. Warmth, compassion, and simple human decency would be the norm; wars, death camps, systematic coercion, and other horrors would become but distant memories. Even ordinary crime would be rare instead of mind-numbingly common.

Could such a world be coaxed into being? Is there any chance for the deepest, most central desire of the human heart to be realized?

Perhaps there is.

This book is about that possibility.

SECTION ONE

THE IDEA OF
PARADISE

CHAPTER 1

THE HUNGER FOR A COMPASSIONATE WORLD

OH, FOR A WORLD OF LOVE AND COMPASSION! A world kind and humane, untainted by crime or hatred! A world of freedom and plenty, with gulags and famine unknown. A world healthy and sane, and real, where human evil is no longer among us, nor remembered, nor conceived.

As newborns, we *expect* such a world. We need it with every cell of our bodies.

Why, then, does it not exist?

– 2 –

THIS BOOK DESCRIBES an idea and provides a collection of data to support that idea. It is also an invitation to participate in the idea, in whatever way appeals to you.

The idea itself is simple. It has only a few components, and you already know most of them. At the center of this idea is something we have all heard before, from many sources: that *love*—compassion for others—*can save the world.*

We have heard that "love can save the world" so often because it is a basic human truth, and because nothing on Earth is more important. Love is the *only* thing that can make the world fully human, just as it is the only thing that can make each of us, individually, fully healthy and human.

But a question arises: if love can save the world, why hasn't it?

Love has not yet saved the world because it needs help. The five-word sentence "Love can save the world" is a compressed version of the truth, and some of the missing detail is important.

In particular, a single, well-documented fact has shaken our faith in the power of love:

Love's *healing* power is far weaker than its power to *prevent* damage in the first place.

In short, only love given early enough in life—and widely enough—can save the world.

— 3 —

THE WORLD does need saving.

In more colorful language, the world is a mess. It is a mess because (as we discuss in later chapters) people are emotionally damaged early in life—by a lack of love, mostly—and the damage stays with them, affecting how they feel, how they think, and how they behave. This damage is passed on, from generation to generation. It affects not only individuals but also groups—families, businesses, towns, nations, and the world as a whole.

None of this is new. It is an ancient problem, as writings from the distant past make clear.

— 4 —

WE HAVE ALWAYS KNOWN that love could save the world, and that nothing else could. Here is another piece of the puzzle that we have always known:

"The Child is father to the Man" [1]

This has been said in many ways. Another example is, "As the twig is bent, so grows the tree."

The modern equivalent is less lyrical but more precise:

*"Complex systems exhibit sensitive dependence
on early conditions."*

Of course, a human being is nothing if not a complex system, even if books on Chaos Theory and Complexity Theory seldom mention this fact.

Early experience is crucial to what we become: happy or miserable; healthy or sick; loving or hateful; trusting or cynical; compassionate or cruel. Early events set the tone for later life. We see and feel the world through the lens of early experience, usually without noticing that the lens is there.

Repairing emotional damage is at best a long and difficult task, and for that reason *preventing* it is the only hope for improving the human condition. Emotional damage can be prevented (or at least reduced) simply and easily, by love and compassion early in life. Even changes in birth practices can have dramatic effects, as Dr. Frederick Leboyer and others have shown.

Love prevents damage, but it does little to *heal* damage that has already set in.

– 5 –

ON A WIDER LEVEL, the character of a society is determined by the character of the people who make up that society. A village (or world) of loving, compassionate adults will not be a village (or world) of war, of crime, of secret mass graves filled on the order of madmen. It will not be a world where armies of emotionally damaged soldiers will be *available* to madmen, or where centralized power over others generally will be seen as acceptable. Nor will such a world need the drugs, legal and otherwise, now used by the trainload to calm the nerves and cover the pain of damaged children who have grown into uneasy adulthood.

Of the many attempts to fix all that—to improve the human condition—none has yet ended war, crime, atrocity, or simple human misery.

What will?

Only one thing: *wide understanding of the cause of the problem, and of the importance of change.*

The *cause* is this: emotional damage early in life leads to damaged adults, who perpetuate the damage to the next generation. Social structures and even large-scale group behaviors are characterized by the people who make up societies. Emotionally damaged people make for damaging societies. Lack of love and other proper care early in life causes the damage.

The *importance* is urgent, compelling, crucial, life-and-death. Individually, each new life is a universe unto itself, and ruining that life (the default in most of today's world) is a tragedy of the greatest magnitude. Globally, the human race is at a critical point: on the verge of extinction at its own hand, or perhaps worse (survival amid the polluted, radioactive wreckage, for example; survival in a universal police state, for another). On the other hand, we could be on the verge of ending war, atrocity, and other human evil—and much ordinary misery besides.

Specifically (and to say it again, for it cannot be said too often): **linking treatment of the young**—of pregnant mothers, babies, infants, and children—**with the character of the world at large** in the minds of people everywhere, will lead to positive changes in attitudes and behavior.

Over time, those changes will improve the world.

Save it, perhaps. Not in an afterlife, you understand: here on Earth. A world of healthy, loving, compassionate human beings would be nothing less than the Paradise that every human infant, and every not-yet-deadened child yearns for—and *has* yearned for, since the beginning. There is nothing supernatural about the concept; nothing unreal, nothing beyond what we see in a truly healthy family or in the eyes of a loved and loving child.

– 6 –

A TASK THIS LARGE requires appropriate tools. Because we are trying to change the thinking and behavior of millions, we need a tool that works on that order of magnitude. We need a tool that works across long spans of time, because the job will not be done in a few months or years.

Such tools are available. They are called **paradigms**.

CHAPTER 2

PARADIGMS:
TOOLS OF PERCEPTION

PARADIGM IS A FANCY WORD FOR "a particular way of viewing reality."* More detailed definitions also exist.

In his classic work <u>The Structure of Scientific Revolutions</u>, Thomas Kuhn developed the idea that paradigms, in the form of widely-shared assumptions, theories, examples, and beliefs, create the intellectual environment in which science can function. Indeed, they create some of the environment in which people and societies function in general. Paradigms give meaning to diverse sets of data. They provide frameworks in which to operate and guide action in useful ways.[2]

Any approach to Paradise must, at a minimum, not violate the idea of Paradise itself. Paradigms fit that rule: they are powerful yet non-coercive; they are decentralized and entirely appropriate to the task.

---

* The word "paradigm" is notoriously difficult to pin down, as Thomas Kuhn himself acknowledged (endnote 2 in this book provides some related detail). The definition given here is a compact synthesis from various dictionaries.

– 2 –

The Power of Paradigms

FOR EXAMPLE, we wash our hands, avoid coughing in people's faces, brush our teeth, use antiseptic on wounds, and vaccinate our children because of a commonly-shared paradigm relating to germs and illness. The result is far less mortality from infectious disease, lower death rates for the young, and even the complete elimination (smallpox) or near-complete elimination (polio, for instance) of diseases that once killed and crippled millions.

– 3 –

THE MODERN IDEA of science is itself a paradigm, and a spectacular one. At its core is the belief that the world is best and most usefully understood by careful, systematic *research*, along with *theory* that is tested against that research. There is more to the scientific method and what might be termed the scientific mindset, of course, and it is this entire collection of standards, beliefs, ideas, rules, and so on that has been so impressive at revealing the depths of nature and at transforming the world.

For centuries, learned men* consulted the writings of ancients rather than perform experiments on physical systems (to discover, for example, the speeds at which two different objects fall). The scientific approach of actually looking at the world to see what happens seems almost too obvious to mention, but for centuries it was largely ignored and out of favor.

Science begat improvement because it involved a more accurate paradigm. Without an accurate paradigm, people will often draw the wrong conclusions *even when relevant facts are well known*. The framework (paradigm) is what makes sense of the facts.

Unfortunately, seeing outside one's current paradigm is almost as difficult as seeing through a concrete wall. Changing one's para-

---

* Women, of course, were seldom involved in such pursuits—another change.

digm is like shifting one's vision to see those hidden 3-D pictures that initially look like random blotches of colors; unless one can focus one's eyes (or mind) just right, the image never comes to life.

– 4 –

How a Simple Paradigm Transformed the World

"TRANSFORMED THE WORLD" is not an overstatement. If anything, it is not forceful enough. Thanks to the paradigm of science, and the sub-paradigm centered around the germ theory of disease, life expectancy in the United States at the end of the twentieth century was roughly *thirty years longer* than at the beginning—people were living, on average, into their seventies instead of their forties. Why? Mostly because vast numbers of people (including a disproportionate number of infants and children) were no longer dying prematurely in horrible, painful ways from infectious disease.[3]

How's that for "changing the world?"

The improvement is more than most of us realize, and perhaps more than any of us today can truly appreciate.

Cholera, yellow fever, dysentery, smallpox, polio, and dozens of other horrors have killed so many, century after century, that for most of history death at a young age was common. Even modestly-sized families typically had at least one child die before puberty. Entire nations and regions could be decimated by plagues. The Black Death, for instance, killed a third of Europe in the space of three or four years.

Scores of diseases have inflicted horrible deaths upon men, women, children, and infants relentlessly throughout human history. The diseases and symptoms have been many and varied, but all have been cruel, both to the victims and to their families and friends. How many children have been orphaned, for example, by diseases over the centuries?

– 5 –

Ten Thousand Years of Death and Misery, Ended By a Paradigm

THE PARADIGM THAT GREW around the germ theory of disease changed all that. Today, deadly epidemics are rare in many parts of the world, and almost unknown in the more developed areas. Few families in such nations go through the horror and the grief of losing a child to illness, much less of losing several. It is unusual for Western children to be orphaned because their parents succumbed to cholera, or to lose a parent to tetanus or other such disease. Most infectious disease is preventable or curable today; excruciating death by microbe is no longer the common death sentence it was in the past.

This is one reason why Paradise has become *possible*—which it was not, for most of our history: less grief and pain; less trauma; more potential emotional health.

Even on the poorer parts of the globe, millions of people are today spared early death, disfigurement, and misery thanks to the same paradigm. Infectious disease has not been eradicated, but it has been clearly and decisively diminished.

– 6 –

Perfection Not Necessary

PARADIGMS CAN BRING about astonishing change even when they are imperfect or incomplete. For that matter, "perfection" is seldom attained in anything, including modern science or medicine— which are constantly filling in gaps and correcting errors with new data. Another example: even the best baseball team or NBA franchise typically loses several games a season. Babe Ruth, Michael Jordan, Venus and Serena Williams, Tiger Woods, and other sports superstars all have far-less than perfect records. Still, no one would call them failures.

Coverage of every relevant factor is not necessary either; a paradigm can be highly effective without being all-inclusive. For instance, there is more to disease than germs: nutrition, stress, poisons in the environment, genetic details of an individual's immune system, and other factors are important. In many diseases, germs play little or no role. Despite that, germ-based diseases have been a plague (thousands of plagues, actually) since the dawn of time—and the germ theory of disease allowed men and women to vastly reduce the death and misery caused by such disease.

The germ theory became the core of a paradigm that allowed mankind to cut infectious disease to a tolerable level. We have not ended infectious disease, and perhaps we never will. But the paradigm has diminished the levels of such disease to a point where the quality of life has improved for literally billions of people.

– 7 –

Many Problems; One Solution

A GOOD PARADIGM can address and solve many seemingly different and intractable problems at once. For example, when the cause of disease was unknown, and because there were dozens of infectious diseases killing thousands on a regular basis, these diseases appeared to be dozens of major and quite distinct problems.

But in some ways, **they are all *one* problem**. The paradigm created by the germ theory taught this new idea to doctors, scientists, and eventually to almost everyone. Some of the resulting actions and remedies worked to reduce the incidence of, or to lessen the severity of, or to prevent altogether, *many diseases at once*. For instance, surgeons began washing their hands to reduce the spread of germs, which greatly reduced infections from a variety of different organisms transmitted during surgery. As mentioned, mothers began to teach their children to wash their hands before meals for the same reason—and to do other things, such as put antibiotic ointment on cuts—with the same positive result: less infectious disease in general; more good health. The problems posed by many seemingly unrelated diseases were addressed by one paradigm.

The germ theory led to many beneficial approaches and behaviors. By creating a new and more useful framework for understanding the problem of infectious disease, it gave natural human problem-solving ability something real to work with.

A usefully accurate paradigm makes all the difference. In this case, the link between microscopic organisms and infectious disease was the key ingredient (but not the only ingredient) in a paradigm that, over time, saved many millions of lives and prevented untold pain and misery.

In the same way, a paradigm which helps people understand the link between [*treatment of the young*] and [*the character of the human world*] will—as it gains wide-enough acceptance—reduce crime, cut drug use, prevent much of the personal misery which *causes* the drug use in the first place, eventually put an end to war, and do other positive things that today seem impossible. Yet I do not believe such things *are* impossible—only that we haven't done them yet.

The elements of the paradigm are, for the most part, already well-known. More than anything else, this book is a way to publicize those elements, to give them a name and a cohesive, concise presence in people's minds—to make them *visible* and to tie them together in hopes they will reach, with the aid of other like-minded people, the necessary critical mass.

Perhaps I am being overly-optimistic, but then again, perhaps not. In any case: suppose all this effort ever does is improve the lives of even a small number of children.

Would that be a bad thing?

– *8* –

Why and How Paradigms Work at Such Magnitude

PARADIGMS WORK by harnessing the natural creativity, intelligence, and energy of millions of people.

By not forcibly imposing a single plan, many plans and approaches may be taken. By not creating a centralized bureaucracy, a paradigm fosters the sincere, diverse efforts of many people.

Paradigms are tools of perception, not coercion.

Paradigms harness the free human action of as many people as care to join in—and nothing formal is required. The mere understanding of a paradigm begins to shape behavior in light of that understanding.

This hints at the first thing anyone can do to advance the goal of a healthier world: spread the word. Tell people that such a world *is* possible, and that proper treatment of pregnant women, infants, and children is the necessary, central tool to get there.

– 9 –

Emergence

THERE IS STILL MORE to the power of paradigms. In particular, there is the phenomenon of *emergence.*[4]

Emergence is the process whereby simple action at one level creates more complex and seemingly unrelated forms and entities at higher levels.

The lower-level actions are performed by micro elements—cells in a body, ants in an anthill, people in a society—that, together, create something entirely different.

Paradigms *reprogram* the micro elements (us) in the emergent system of human society. That is, paradigms change people's thinking in ways that lead to changes in actions, and thus to changes in the larger system that emerges from those actions.

Lower-level action; higher-level result.

– 10 –

Astonishing Creative Power

AS NOTED, the higher-order structures in emergent systems are different in kind from the lower-order activity that gives rise to them.

For instance, animals are more than the cells in their bodies. Your dog is not simply a larger version of a dog cell; it is an entirely new type of thing, made up, yes, of cells containing canine DNA, but completely unlike those cells in most ways. Your dog *emerges* from the action of its cells, somewhat in the way that *music* emerges from a player reading data on a Compact Disk.

Consider the emergent system of a human being. Individual cells—too small to see with the naked eye, and without anything we would normally consider "intelligence"—become a sophisticated, fully-functioning multicelled organism, in this case, a human being, including human consciousness. This person's cells manage to create different organ systems, repair cellular damage, heal wounds, fight infectious disease, discard waste, draw useful energy from food and air, and do many other quite amazing things.

How? By obeying the simple, lower-level rules (which often involve reacting to local conditions) that guide individual cellular behavior. This behavior does something you or I could never do "scientifically" with even the best current knowledge: build a living organism from the ground up and operate it for a lifetime, including designing it to self-reproduce before it wears out.

– *11* –

To Succeed With a Complex System, Decentralize

IMAGINE IF EACH CELL in your body had to check in with your brain before taking action in response to changes in the environment, or to its own needs.

> Cell 472340-A93 in Left Kidney Sector to Brain: Slight increase in local acidity. Should action be taken? If so, what? Please advise.

The human body contains 100 trillion cells or more, and one easily sees how centralized control on such a level would fail, quickly and catastrophically. Of course, the brain *does* monitor and respond to bodily conditions, but generally on a far larger scale—it responds, in most cases, to what might be termed gross changes in condition rather than to changes at the level of an individual cell.

If trillions of cells were constantly passing information to the brain about every little change in their environments and their internal status, and then getting a useful response, the bandwidth required (in each direction!) would far exceed the organism's capacity. For that matter, the processing power required for the brain to evaluate and accurately respond to such an avalanche of requests, even assuming they could be delivered reliably and in a timely fashion, would be staggering.

In a truly complex and rapidly changing system, local information requires *local* detection, decision, and action for consistently appropriate and accurate response.

This is not to say that some level of centralized direction and control is always useless or bad policy, but rather to point out that large, complex, emergent systems are—by definition, and for reasons built-in to the nature of things—*not* run from the top down. Instead, as the term implies, they emerge from the bottom up.

Not surprisingly, our cells make their own decisions about most things, leaving the brain to handle more global issues. Were this not so, I would not be alive to write these words, nor you to read them.

– 12 –

SOCIAL INSECTS are among the best-known examples of the decentralized nature of emergence. Individual bees are not very intelligent, yet a hive of bees behaves in an intelligent and complex fashion. The guiding intelligence for those actions does *not* come from the queen or from any other individual insect. There is no centralized power structure—no cabinet-level agencies, no power-hungry bees striving to "rule the world"—in a beehive.

The same is true for ants: they don't go to ant college or look to some Maximum Leader to learn how to forage for food, to tend the young, to defend the nest, or to do anything else. Instead, they behave instinctively, based on simple rules. The entire civilization of each ant species emerges from individual ants, interacting with other individual ants and with their immediate environment. There *is* no "ant leader," no central authority, no ant bureaucracy, no method for centralized control at all.

How, then, does the sophisticated society of an ant or bee

species emerge?

The simple answer is this: It emerges because *sophisticated higher-level behavior emerging from simple, rule-based, decentralized lower-level behavior is a common, built-in feature of the universe itself.* Like gravity or the rules of quantum physics, *emergence* (of higher-level order from certain types of lower-level rule-based behavior) is a basic law of nature.

– 13 –

GIVEN THE POWER of emergence in creating and shaping large systems, it requires no great leap of faith to believe that, properly harnessed, paradigms—programming tools for the emergent system of human society—could create a more compassionate world.

Indeed, no other tool or method seems a viable candidate for the job. If we want a healthier, saner, and more compassionate world, we must take the complex and emergent nature of human society into account—not fight against it. Efforts which ignore the fundamental nature of the human world—centralized, coercive methods in particular—are doomed to failure.

CHAPTER 3

THE PARADISE PARADIGM

THE THESIS OF THIS BOOK IS THAT the human condition itself—individually and collectively—can be improved dramatically, over time, by increasing the understanding that proper early care leads to a healthier and more compassionate adulthood, and that a society of healthy people will be a healthy society.

Going one step further, a world of healthier societies must, in fact, be a healthier world.

I call this set of ideas the **Paradise Paradigm.** A name is necessary, because it is difficult to talk about something we don't have a name for.

Note that I am not only talking about the need to raise one's own children well, or even to help other children in some manner. I am, in particular, advancing the idea that **only** the widest possible understanding of a *paradigm* on this topic, and an *accurate* one, will succeed at widely improving and eventually "saving" the world in the sense discussed in these pages.

– 2 –

IN MORE DETAIL, the Paradigm has seven points. They are:

1. The human world is as we make it.

2. The character of each adult is largely shaped in the earliest months and years of life.

3. Consistent love and respect given early in life create healthy, loving adults who respect others.

4. Any person or group which improves the lives of pregnant mothers, infants, or children contributes to the goal of a healthy world. To a lesser extent, improving the life of *any* person contributes to the goal.

5. Enough healthy, loving adults will make a healthy, loving world.

6. Freedom is a necessary part of love. Unfreedom (coercion) is abuse; it erodes and destroys love.

7. Change happens when enough people share the necessary understanding.

– 3 –

A brief commentary on each point in turn:

THE HUMAN WORLD IS AS WE MAKE IT. *(Point One)*

This point is two-fold: first, much of the human world is in terrible shape. Second, we have the means to change that—not overnight, of course, but soon enough. Mankind no longer has to put up with widespread violence, racism, and other human evil and misery.

That the human world is "as we make it" seems obvious, but we don't always keep the obvious in mind. Knowing and acting upon the truth that *we can bring about change* is crucial. We *can* make the world as we want it to be, if enough of us understand what we want and how to get there.

To put it bluntly, the world can be healed. We can make this Earth a Paradise.

What does that mean: "a Paradise?"

It means a world without wars, without crime against others, without *needless* misery.

Can we create such a world? Of course we can. This book is designed to spread the idea that such a world is possible, and to remind people of what they already know: how to get there.

Note that I am *not* using the word "Paradise" in a supernatural or conventionally religious sense. As used here, it does not mean any place, in heaven or elsewhere, where we might find ourselves after death. Nor is it meant to suggest that the world can be made "perfect" or completely without pain, misery, or even conflict.

Instead, I see "Paradise" as simply *a world without human evil.* My premise is that the worst of what we read about in our newspapers, and that we find in our history books, can, should, and must be eliminated from the world.

How? *By raising enough emotionally-healthy children to create a healthy world.* To start, that means *spreading the idea that it can be done,* and that loving, compassionate treatment of the young—of pregnant mothers, newborns, infants, and children—is the method with which to address the problem.

— *4* —

HOW LONG WILL IT TAKE to accomplish such a goal? No one can say, of course, and the shock of merely considering such a question suggests what we are up against. But I am convinced that real, visible progress could take only a few decades, were we to begin the process now and in earnest. Full success, of course, will take longer, no matter how earnest and efficient we are: generations, in fact. This is not a short-term project.

Nor is *perfection* an option. Some people may still be rude—but do they have to be murderers, rapists, or con artists? Some of us may be unhappy, even with the most loving and gentle of childhoods—but must any of us be genocidal dictators? Or their henchmen? Must any of us (or at least so very many of us) be depressed or addicted or thoughtless or cruel?

Many will find this hard to accept, but please consider that it is *time to end human evil*—and along the way, to eliminate much of human misery besides. Indeed, we may not have much time left to make the transition to a more gentle and emotionally healthy world. Modern technology brings enough danger that this, right now, could be our only chance to get things right.

Now or never.

– 5 –

WHAT IS EVIL?

As with "Paradise," the term "evil" in this framework means something different than the traditional supernatural or religious concept. This book takes no position whatever on the existence or nature of hell, Satan, or any other religious concept or belief.

Regardless of any supernatural concept of evil, it is possible to define and identify *human* evil and, more importantly, to begin and encourage the process of ending it.

The definition of evil used throughout this book:

Human evil is the end result of infants and newborns (and even "preborns") being made repressed, unfeeling, and angry by a childhood, and then a lifetime, of pain. In short, *evil is people hurt so badly that they, in turn, hurt others needlessly.*

In my view, evil is that and nothing else.

– 6 –

EVERY CRIMINAL ACT, from petty assault to genocide, begins with damage done to the perpetrator very early in life. Every criminal is also a victim; every evil soul was once an innocent babe.

No child is born a murderer. No infant is genetically destined to be a rapist or a con-man or a psychopathic killer. If genetics were the answer here, we would be hunting down the genes involved, doing tests, and using the results to prevent the mass murderers and career criminals of tomorrow. But while genes may predispose us to certain behaviors—including toward violent behavior, poor impulse-control, and drug addiction—the expression of those tendencies in a truly damaging way is caused by environmental factors—by experiences during birth, infancy, and early childhood. And yes, in the womb.

Love cannot usually save an adult who is already sociopathic, and a loving environment may or may not improve the life and behavior of a neurotic adult.

But love can and does prevent babies, infants, and very young children from becoming sociopathic—or chronically miserable, for that matter. Connection to others, respect for others, and deep feeling itself is our natural state, but only when we are loved, cared for, and respected at the very start of our lives.

There is an ocean of scientific evidence to support this, and this book references some of that evidence. But do you need someone in a lab coat to tell you that infants need loving, gentle treatment? Is there any doubt in your mind that treating infants (or puppies, for that matter) with love produces loving adults, or that treating them with callousness, violence, anger, or neglect produces—must produce—unhappy and possibly violent adults?

In the end, this is less a scientific issue than a human one. Think for yourself, please, and trust your own heart.

– 7 –

THE CHARACTER OF EACH ADULT IS LARGELY SHAPED IN THE EARLIEST MONTHS AND YEARS OF LIFE. *(Point Two)*

I mentioned two Western epigrams on the topic earlier:

"The child is father to the man"
and
"As the twig is bent, so grows the tree."

The modern understanding that complex systems show "sensitive dependence on early conditions" only confirms and expands upon what we have known for millennia. Events early in the life of a complex system tend to have far more impact on the outcome or later states of that system, than do similar events which happen at a later time.

Other things being equal, early experience is more powerful than later experience, and the changes wrought by early experience become the foundation that later character and experience must be built upon.

– 8 –

CONSISTENT LOVE AND RESPECT GIVEN EARLY IN LIFE CREATE HEALTHY, LOVING ADULTS WHO RESPECT OTHERS. *(Point Three)*

This should be obvious; it is also a corollary to something we read about frequently: that abused children often grow up to be abusive adults.

It isn't always "someone else" who is being abused, either. Many abused children grow up to abuse themselves, with unhealthy and destructive habits. Smoking, heavy drinking, and the use of other drugs are all higher among adults who were abused as children. Not surprisingly, cancer, heart disease, and other physical problems are also more common among such adults.

The good news is that a loving childhood—starting with good prenatal care, and continuing through birth, infancy, and later childhood—sets the stage for a life with less risk of physical and emotional problems. In addition to the studies and anecdotal evidence for this (that is, in addition to studies and other evidence phrased in positive ways), every "negative" study which shows that abused children are more likely to become violent or abusive adults, is also saying that loved, non-abused children have a better chance at a normal, loving, non-abusive later life.

– 9 –

ANY PERSON OR GROUP WHICH IMPROVES THE LIVES OF
PREGNANT MOTHERS, INFANTS, AND CHILDREN, CONTRIBUTES
TO THE GOAL OF A HEALTHY WORLD. *(Point Four)*

This is intuitive, obvious—and important. A healthy human world
will never emerge while large numbers of humans are repressed,
traumatized, and without a sense of love and connection to others.
**To a lesser extent, improving the life of *any person* also con-
tributes to the goal.** More compassion, more love, more
emotionally healthy interaction even among the elderly, among
non-parents, and among fathers are clearly good things in and of
themselves. Improving the world ahead requires, in particular, that
the *young* be treated well, but everyone deserves to be treated with
respect and compassion. Furthermore, even adults who have little
contact with children often have *some* contact with them or affect
children indirectly.

– 10 –

ENOUGH HEALTHY, LOVING ADULTS WILL MAKE A HEALTHY,
LOVING WORLD. *(Point Five)*

This is simple mathematics. Who are the bad guys gonna get to run
the concentration camps and staff the secret police, when almost
everyone is emotionally healthy? Who will be the executioner,
when every person feels love in their heart for others? How often
will crimes be committed against others when no one was victim-
ized during childhood?
Perhaps it is time to find out.

– 11 –

FREEDOM IS A NECESSARY PART OF LOVE. UNFREEDOM (COER-
CION) IS ABUSE; IT ERODES AND DESTROYS LOVE. *(Point Six)*

"IMPROVING THE LIVES OF THE YOUNG" includes letting them live
in freedom rather than under tyranny, in both the political and

personal sense. Freedom is necessary in our daily, personal lives as well as in our social and political structures.

Children are small and weak compared to adults, and are often treated with authoritarianism—that is, they are not allowed much freedom. It is all-too-easy for an adult to be a tyrant with a child, and this is more prevalent than most of us care to believe.

Being denied freedom and thus responsibility in childhood makes it less likely that one will understand freedom and responsibility as an adult. Not being shown respect during childhood makes it less likely that we will respect others. In short, love without freedom is at best incomplete.

– 12 –

CHANGE HAPPENS WHEN ENOUGH PEOPLE SHARE THE NECESSARY UNDERSTANDING. *(Point Seven)*

Why? Because that is how paradigms work, as we saw in the previous chapter.

– 13 –

LET US BE CLEAR on the Paradise Paradigm's major point: we can literally save the world—make it far more healthy and human than we ever thought possible—by simply spreading the truth that raising enough emotionally-healthy children will create a healthy world.

When enough people understand the link between early experience and the human condition, the shift toward ending the dark age will begin, because belief systems guide behavior.

What will that mean, exactly? We cannot know the details ahead of time, since human society is inherently chaotic and its details unpredictable.[5] Perhaps churches will devote less energy to bingo and more to helping young parents. Perhaps the trend toward gentle birth begun by Frederick Leboyer will accelerate and such births will become the norm. There are thousands of ways that people and groups can act to bring about this new world. All we can know for certain is that movement in the right direction will eventually take us where we want to go.

– *14* –

OF COURSE, it must also be said that if success is a realistic possible outcome, so is failure. It may be too late, or we humans too perverse, for anything to put an end to hatred, war, racism, crime, and other needless misery. Perhaps even love cannot save the world, after all.

Many will say so.

My response is: so what? What is the downside of loving children instead of beating and humiliating and neglecting and otherwise abusing them?

How bad could it be to simply treat infants and children with love, care, and respect?

If it doesn't save the world, at least it will help one child at a time.

For those who would not dream of treating a child in any other fashion than with love, care, and respect, I again emphasize that **saving the world requires more than raising one's own children well: it requires creating, fostering, and widely disseminating a new paradigm.** *One* child raised with love creates a single healthy adult, which is a good thing, of course, but is not enough to save the world. There are hundreds of millions of other children, and most are less fortunate.

To change the world, we must change the way people think about babies, infants, and children. People must know that *an important and world-wide change can and will come from society-wide improvements in the care of the young.*

The change will come *only* from that; nothing else will do. There is no techno-magic we can substitute, nor any spiritual game we can play to do the job. Real infants have real needs, and the changes we seek will only come when we meet those real needs appropriately, consistently, and routinely, on the widest possible scale. And for that, we must create and advance a new paradigm.

− 15 −

Enough "movement in the right direction" will in fact transform the human world, even more dramatically than we have transformed it with technology. This transformation—I would, of course, call it the Paradise Transformation—*has already begun.* The only questions are how quickly and optimally the transformation will proceed, and whether we will complete it in time. Time *is* an issue because mankind will not long survive the combination of widespread emotional damage, powerful modern technologies, and the use of coercion (government force) to run entire societies.

− 16 −

HOW IMPORTANT is all this? It is critical. I cannot imagine anything as urgent, as important, as profoundly necessary.

The truth of this may be hard to grasp. That is what our defenses are for—keeping painful truths away from us. Besides, much of the world seems fine, and there are millions of decent, warm, kind-hearted people.

The good in life makes it easy to tell ourselves that nothing is wrong. Besides, what can we do about society-wide, even world-wide problems? It isn't just crime and genocide that we are talking about. It is "the human condition," including the inner states that cause the crime in the first place—and which cause misery even where no crime is being committed.

This is about the too-common state of neurosis, of repressed feeling, of tension and anxiety and psychosomatic symptoms of every type. I am talking about the near-universal human distress that fuels the tobacco industry, the alcohol industry, the cocaine industry, and all the trade in other drugs that people use to feel better, to blot the pain, to numb themselves and free themselves, if for only a moment and imperfectly, from what psychologist Arthur Janov calls "the lifetime sentence." This isn't something minor; by some estimates, people spend more money on illegal drugs world-wide than they do on food.[6]

I am talking about child abuse and wife-beating and gang warfare; about genocide and death camps; about the tics and compulsions and headaches and unreal worries of the average adult. I am speaking of free-floating paranoia and chronic depression, of suicide and frigidity and racism and sneaky office politics and the endless, sorry litany of pain and neurosis we try our best to ignore, to hide from, to wish out of existence.

I swear to you: *none of this has to be*. Not in the long term, anyway. We cannot wave our hands and make things better, of course, and making things better for an already-suffering adult is a long and difficult task. Nothing, in fact, can make us what we might have been.

But the process of destroying new lives can be stopped. The problem can be solved, and solved permanently. Our grandchildren and their grandchildren will inherit a vastly different world. Why not a healthier and more human world as well?

As long as enough potential dictators, death-camp guards, and other violent criminals exist, the rest of us will be in danger. As long as a huge pool of potential "followers" can be turned into armies that will follow evil orders without question, we will have wars and atrocities. As long as deprived, neurotic parents are inflicting deprivation and pain on new generations, the dark age will continue, as it has for thousands of years.

For each person, there is no substitute for love at an early age.

For every society, there is no substitute for a near-complete majority of healthy, loving adults.

For mankind, there is no substitute for a world composed of healthy people, societies, and nations.

A world of violence, neurosis, and psychopathology is a tragedy at any time. But tomorrow's mass killing won't involve only swords or small arms: it will, eventually, involve tens of thousands of nuclear-tipped missiles. It will involve cleverly engineered bio-weapons. It will involve, more than likely, horrors we cannot even imagine—yet.

Now or never.

– 17 –

HOW, EXACTLY, would all this work?

It is important to understand that we are not talking about large, centrally controlled structures such as government programs. As we saw in the previous chapter, paradigms are the opposite of centralized methods; there is no "paradigm headquarters," no "President of the Paradigm." A paradigm is simply the widespread understanding that things work in a particular way; useful action and results flow from that understanding, instead of from edicts, five-year plans, or laws.

What can you, or any one person, really do to help change the world? Simply understanding the basic idea is a good start, and if you've reached this page, you've probably done that already. Because paradigmatic change requires wide understanding of the paradigm, helping to spread the word is an obvious and important way to participate in advancing the goal of a healthier world. Pass this book along to a friend after you finish it for example, and email the URL for the companion website (*http://www.paradise-paradigm.net*) to someone.

Big plans and heroic efforts are not needed; or rather, those who feel they are needed will do them. We will each do what we are drawn to do. Jonas Salk invented the first polio vaccine; that was a major effort and a spectacular success, in terms of preventing disease. Mothers and fathers simply took the family down to be vaccinated—and did other things, usually, to protect their families from germ-borne illness. All of it together—big, coordinated efforts and small individual actions—was needed to solve the problem.

Those actions, big and small, were effective at reducing the toll from infectious disease. Of course, the results have not been perfect. That is, we are not finished, and our efforts have not been without problem and failure. But polio is nearly gone from most of the world, and germ-based disease generally is so diminished as a human problem that the resulting population explosion has become a new problem to be solved.*

In short, the power of paradigms comes from their ability to enlist the energy and creativity of many, many individuals—by not forcing the issue, by not being rigid; by nothing more than providing a framework for looking at and thinking about the problem clearly.

Paradigms help large numbers of people share the same basic understanding. In turn, these people provide solutions and work-arounds and insights and energy, in the service of solving the problem or dealing with the situation appropriately. When enough people share the paradigm, this all happens automatically. Hard work may be needed, and time, but a central authority is not.

Many individual minds are smarter than one mind.

Many hearts, followed in earnest, can keep a group or society on the right path.

– *18* –

THE PARADISE PARADIGM grew out of my desire for a healthier, more compassionate world—even if I won't be around to see it completed. This book was written to awaken your own desire for the same thing: for a world with more love and compassion; a world with less violence and pain. If enough people are moved by the idea that the world could be healed (saved, changed for the better, improved, or however you prefer to think of it)—then their behavior will change in accordance with that desire.

The Paradise Paradigm says that "love can save the world." It is people, of course, who will do the saving. It is people—millions of them, eventually, if we are to succeed—who will find ways to improve their own behavior towards their own children, or to improve the lives of groups of children, or to cajole their churches into helping insure that pregnant mothers in the congregation get proper nutrition. It is people who will decide to express compassion; to make some part of the world, large or small, more decent and kind and free and sane.

---

* It is critical to note that *lack of perfection* has not prevented the germ theory paradigm from *literally changing the world.*

Their actions will echo deep into the future.

The children who benefit today (and *their* children, and their children) will grow to adulthood. When enough healthy adults inhabit the world, the world itself will be healthy. This may sound too obvious to express, but it is the heart of the matter. Are you tired of hearing that some madman sent an army of sociopathic soldiers to systematically rape and kill innocent civilians somewhere? I certainly am. Then know that nothing else will solve the problem, except replacing repressed, emotionally damaged adults with healthy, compassionate adults.

And doing that, of course, requires compassionate treatment of pregnant mothers, infants, and children. Of, eventually, all of them. There are no shortcuts.

When enough of us have made the connection between **early experience** and **adult character and behavior,** and also fully grasped that enough emotionally healthy adults will make a healthy world, then change will happen. In fact, at that point, it will be unstoppable.

The actions people take won't always be visible or dramatic. They won't even always be helpful. But in ways large and small, people will begin to act consistently with the idea that *more compassion early in life creates healthier, happier, and more compassionate adults.* They will act, sometimes, from a desire to improve the lives of individual children and the adults those children will become. They will act, in many cases, from a desire to help make a healthier, less violent world. They will act in their own ways, for their own reasons.

And that is how the world is changed.

– *19* –

SIMPLE UNDERSTANDING is, once again, the start of the process. I encourage you to step inside the idea, look around, and begin to see and feel the extent to which this world could be made better—*must* be made better. Getting beyond the sense that this is "too big a job," or that even thinking about such change is silly, is only a barrier to understanding. Another is the refusal to see the need for change;

it hurts to see the world as it is, and for that reason, we seldom do.

Before you finish this volume, you will, I hope, have moved beyond that, to the point where a new world—the world as it really *can* be—is a reality in your mind and in your heart. More than that, I hope you will sometimes feel the loss of that world; that you will grieve at having been denied it; feel sadness and anger on behalf of others. I am convinced that we all long for a world of compassion, freedom, and brotherhood. The haunting image of that world lives, literally, within our DNA. We are genetically programmed for such a world, just as we are programmed to eat, to breathe, and to communicate. Love, freedom, and connection with others are what we expect, what we crave, what we are born for.

We spend our lives hiding from our own disappointment at their lack.

Changing the world sounds impossible, but the world changes anyway. Humankind is on the cusp of a metamorphosis beyond anything we have experienced; everyone knows as much. The twentieth century moved from the horse and buggy to the passenger jet and the space station, from the telegraph to the World Wide Web. The next hundred years will bring far greater transformations. Guessing at them is a modern cottage industry.

The characteristics of this change are at issue. One current trend (towards more centralized power) could lead to a global police state; at the extreme, it could create a global concentration camp, as Marxism helped to create nation-states in the image of concentration camps in Pol Pot's Cambodia, in North Korea, in Red China, in the Soviet Union, and elsewhere.

But there are opposing trends, and my hope is to encourage and strengthen them. The gift we can offer future generations (and to some extent our own) is a world with more love and compassion, a world of people who sense their connection with others, and with all life. A world with less coercion and more respect for human rights. It won't be a "perfect" world, of course, because perfection is not an option. But we should not let that keep us from considering and striving for what we truly want: a healthier, less repressed and repressive, and more deeply *human* world.

Such change can happen. Indeed, change itself is unstoppable; it is all around us, a hurricane of glistening transformation, reshaping our world as we watch. "Sensitive dependence on early conditions" is dripping from every crack and pore in the modern world. Small inputs, of the right kind, can have a powerful and positive impact far into the future.

The right input is crucial.

CHAPTER 4

THE NEW WORLD

THE PARADISE PARADIGM says that we can change the character of society, and of the people who make up society, forever. You may be wondering if such a sea change is really possible.

It may help to consider another world-changing event, and the paradigm shift linked with it, that we are all familiar with: the discovery by Europeans of the New World, in the late 1400s. The results of this event have been mixed, of course, but there is no denying the power and scope of the changes.

Imagine, if you will, the complete transformation of today's modern world, backward in time half a millennium, to a world without a single electrical appliance, without automobiles, without trains, without steam engines. We could be anywhere on the Earth, but it happens that we are in Europe, perhaps in Spain or Italy. Imagine awaking each day into a world without modern dentistry or medicine, without telephones or even a telegraph. Let the transformation sink in for a moment; feel yourself there, in this long-ago yet far-from-ancient time. Hear the horses in the streets, smell the horse manure and the garbage slopped into the road, see the textures and materials of your fifteenth-century house, visit, in your mind, your kitchen and pantry. You are in the Old World of five centuries ago, where nearly everything we depend upon *today* is yet to be. Change is glacially slow and actively opposed—often violently and cruelly—by both the Church and the State.

What happened, then, to bring the change that created today's *modern* world? Many things, of course. We will focus here, as mentioned, on a single facet of that change: the explorations that led, unexpectedly, to the Americas.

– 2 –

BEFORE THE OLD WORLD could discover the new one, and before it could even conceive such a thing, people had to first discover something else: the courage to believe and to act upon a heresy—a new paradigm. After all, the Earth was flat and at the center of God's universe.[7] Anyone could see that. Almost nothing suggested otherwise; there were no satellite photos of the Earth, no orbiting telescopes, no computers to help analyze Earth-gathered data.

Explorers who questioned the dogma and began their journeys faced terrible difficulties. They had no radio, no radar, and no refrigeration. They had no vaccines or antibiotic medicine. No power sources but human sweat and the fickle wind. They launched their ships, of course, without the detailed maps we take for granted; Columbus arrived at Cuba thinking it was Asia.[8]

Acting on such an idea, by setting out beyond the horizon in a crude wooden ship, was more dangerous than most of us can imagine. With none of the electrical, medical, or other technology we now take for granted, these early explorers were perhaps more foolhardy than brave. Yet they overcame both their natural fear and the cultural dogmas and superstitions they had been drenched in from childhood. Sea monsters, demons of the deep, falling off the edge of the world: these were enough to frighten off most men of the time from such a pursuit.

And those weren't even the real dangers. The real dangers were worse. Malnutrition and starvation; scurvy, infection, dehydration. Wild storms and squalls, or no wind and a becalmed ship. Shipwreck. Mutiny.

The eventual success of these explorations, by men such as Christopher Columbus and Ferdinand Magellan, brought Europeans into the New World and thereby changed the world forever.

– 3 –

MODERN TECHNOLOGY shows us that the Earth is, indeed, a ball spinning in space—but modern technology was five hundred years away in 1492. Worse, challenging official views on scientific topics could result in sanctions. In 1633, more than a century after Columbus sailed, Galileo was sentenced to life in prison for, among other things, maintaining that the Earth orbits the sun. His sentence was commuted to house arrest; others weren't so lucky.

Yet for those with careful eyes, the truth was obvious. For example, in regards the shape of the Earth: watch a ship moving over the horizon. The lower part of the vessel disappears from view first, then, gradually, the sails and masts. Human nature is such that a thousand people can stare truth in the face, and see nothing. One sees what one is ready to see.

– 4 –

COLUMBUS DISCOVERED a continent. He was searching for a quicker trade route to Asia, but found instead new land—a New World, as it came to be known.

There is another New World, of a different kind, and its impact will be even greater. This world is waiting, silently, for us to infer its existence, to calculate its distance and direction, and to come and make it our own. Not only has this New World waited for us, unchanging, but we for it. Centuries have passed, ages and millennia have passed; still this newest and oldest of New Worlds awaits.

There are actually two "New Worlds" involved here. One, of course, is a society—a world-wide society of unique cultures, where compassion has become the norm in every village and city, and where that single thread unites every nation. But for such a world to emerge, another must be found first, deeper and more intimate.

Because this other New World is elusive, many do not believe it exists. It cannot be seen, for it is not a place. It has no landscape and no shoreline; satellite cameras will never capture its image.

Yet this New World is the birthright of every man and woman, of every child. We sense it, faintly, in our dreams. We hear it, sometimes, in music. We see it in the faces and movements of children.

This newest and oldest of worlds lives within us. It is our truest nature and our deepest reality.

Our ancestors buried this world within themselves to survive, eons ago. They did this without knowing or planning. The process was instinctive and unconscious.

It still is.

– 5 –

TIME ROLLS ON; a hundred years will pass soon enough, whether we decide to save the world or not. If we begin the process now, if we begin giving people a framework to see and understand what is at stake and reminding them of what must be done, the next hundred years could bring real progress. Consider how remarkable that would be: In six thousand years of human history nothing has yet improved what we in the West call "the human condition." Despite our science and technology, evil and misery continue. War, murder, rape, and other crime have not stopped. Mass murder of civilians even by educated, "civilized" nations has not stopped either; technology has made it more efficient.

Technology has failed here because *evil and pain are not technological problems.* They are, instead, human problems, and they require human solutions.

A few generations spent taking care of infants and children, including reducing the role of coercion in society, will do what all the technology in the world cannot: put an end to mankind's long dark age of repression, pain, and violence.

All it takes is for enough people to see and understand. The paradigm, if shared widely enough, *will* change the world—because that is what paradigms do.

Less coercion and early pain =
Less neurosis and violence =
A more loving, healthy,
and compassionate world.

SECTION TWO

UNDERSTANDING PARADISE

CHAPTER 5

SENSITIVE DEPENDENCE
ON EARLY CONDITIONS

*It would seem that given a good start in life, almost any kind of
stress can be withstood later on.*

— *Arthur Janov*[9]

THE "NATURE VERSUS NURTURE" argument has persisted for
decades: do our genetics define our character, and thus our
actions, or does our environment shape us instead?[10]

Of course, the answer must be "both, to some extent." The
question (given that most of us are not geneticists) is really, then,
"to what extent does our environment shape us"—or, to ask it
another way, "to what extent can we improve lives, and the human
condition generally, by improving that environment?"

As we shall see in this chapter, the answer to that question is, at
the least: "to a very large extent."

I believe the correct answer is closer to this: "beyond our wildest
dreams."

– 2 –

MANY BOOKS, and thousands of articles and studies, provide detailed discussions of this topic. The goal in this chapter is to provide a short overview, giving a sense of the importance of early experience and providing a sample of the data. References in the Endnotes and in the "Further Reading" section will give readers who want more material a place to find it. The companion website also contains reference material, including, in many cases, direct links to the original documents or to book reviews at Amazon.com and else-where. The page most relevant to this chapter is:

http://www.paradise-paradigm.net/science.htm.

Many studies that support the premise of sensitivity to early con-ditions are reported in daily newspapers, in popular news magazines, and on television. A particular study may have been published in the *Journal of the American Medical Association,* for example, but it may also be summarized in *USA Today* and other popular newspapers. I encourage readers to keep their eyes open for such material; there is more of it than many people probably imagine.

– 3 –

THREE STUDIES REPORTED IN 2000 combine to illuminate this chapter's thesis especially well. In the first, Lane Strathearn, a researcher at Mater Children's Hospital in Brisbane, Australia found that babies with extremely low birthweight (usually due to premature birth) are much more likely to develop learning and lan-guage difficulties in childhood. This fits with other studies that have shown greater chance of various problems developing among premature and low birthweight babies.[11]

Another study of premature infants, this time by Dr. Michael Kramer of McGill University in Montreal, and reported in the *Journal of the American Medical Association,* found that even slightly prema-ture babies were much more likely to die in the first year after birth than full-term infants. Even babies born at 34 to 36 weeks (37 weeks is not generally considered premature) were three times as likely to die in the first year, and for babies born at 32 or 33 weeks, the danger of dying was *six* times normal. Despite those numbers, most doctors are apparently unaware of the dangers, and many births are induced prematurely, often for the convenience of the doctor.[12]

The third item is even more surprising: a National Institutes of Health study of 3,000 pregnant women in Alabama found that mothers with severe gum disease are more likely—by a factor of eight—to have underweight premature babies. Why? It turns out that dental plaque contains prostaglandin—the very substance used to induce labor in hospitals, and which naturally helps induce labor at full term.[13]

In short: *gum disease* in the pregnant mother can cause babies to be born underweight and premature.

In turn, these babies are more at risk for all sorts of later problems, including learning difficulties and even early death.

– 4 –

"SENSITIVE DEPENDENCE on early conditions" sounds remote and technical. Where human lives are concerned, however, it is anything but. Early events are direct, powerful, and often central to the quality, and sometimes the length, of one's life.

Because early events and conditions affect a person's later character and behavior, they also affect the lives of others around that person. In particular, children are affected by the echoes of their parents' early experience. If the parents' early experience was warm, loving, and appropriate, then their children will likely have a warm, loving, and appropriate childhood. The more a parent was traumatized in childhood, however, the more likely that his or her *child's* experience will be traumatic also.

This transmission of trauma from generation to generation is complex and not always obvious to those involved, but it is nonetheless real and powerful. Children are traumatized (and made neurotic) by their parents' neurosis. In this way, the curse of neurosis—of trauma leading to repressed* feeling, and to the myriad behaviors that such repression engenders—has been passed from generation to generation, since before written history began.[14]

That is exactly what one would expect, given what we know about complex systems. Chaos Theory and Complexity Theory, which describe how complex systems evolve, show the power of early experience in shaping later life. They show how difficult it is to pinpoint exactly what the effect will be of an early event, while at the same time revealing the *extent* to which such events create the ultimate character of the system.

Of course, books on Chaos Theory and Complexity Theory seldom discuss how individual human beings are affected by early events,[15] but the core insight of these theories—that extremely complex systems are very sensitive to what happens early in their development—clearly applies, and powerfully, to individual human lives. Each person begins as a tiny blob of DNA from the fusion of a mere two cells; nine months later, if all goes well, we emerge as full-term babies—consisting of many, many billions of cells. After birth we continue to grow rapidly (far more rapidly than we ever will again), so that what happens during infancy or early childhood tends to be *imprinted on new physical, emotional, and mental growth*, and to color how later events are experienced.

– 5 –

A SIMPLE EXAMPLE: a young child has a puppy. The two become good friends, and the child experiences warm and pleasant feelings whenever he or she meets another dog. The child associates "dogs" with consistent love and affection, which the child receives from his or her own dog. Hence, the experience of seeing or meeting a friendly dog is a positive one for the child.

---

* It hardly seems necessary to support the idea of repression of feeling, but in January 2004 the journal *Science* reported a study which used functional magnetic resonance imaging to essentially catch the brain in the act of repressing memory.

Now consider another child, with no pet at home, attacked by a dog and injured or at least badly frightened at an early age. Will *this* child enjoy meeting new dogs? Probably not. This child associates "dogs" with violence, pain, and terror. Regardless of how friendly they are, dogs are now objects of fear to this child, unless and until the traumatic earlier experience is over-ridden by many other positive ones.

In short, our two hypothetical children will have very different experiences when meeting a new dog—even when meeting the *same* dog at the *same time*. A single objective reality—encountering a dog on a walk, in this case—becomes a very different *experience* for the two children, based upon earlier events.

Early experience colors later experience. Given enough seriously bad experience very early in life, almost *every* later experience can be "bad."

This is one reason why prevention of emotional damage is the *only* way in which the human condition will be improved: the earlier damage *creates more damage, even among new experiences* which, without the earlier trauma, would not be damaging. An inherently neutral or potentially pleasant *event* (e.g., meeting a dog on a walk) can become a traumatic *experience*, solely on the basis of earlier painful experience.

The child traumatized early on may thereafter be traumatized more often than he or she otherwise would be, because events that would not normally be traumatic *have become so*, based on the earlier experience. The child is predisposed to be afraid (or angry, or hurt in some fashion) in response to events that would not trigger such feeling in a less-damaged child.[16]

This on-going accretion of painful, unpleasant, or even traumatic *experience* (of objectively non-traumatic *events*) becomes *itself* an increasing source of emotional damage—to the child unfortunate enough to have been made overly sensitive to it.

– 6 –

INTERESTINGLY, HEALTH BENEFITS of love to children often accrue to the mother, as well as to the child. For example, a recent article in the medical journal *Lancet*[17] showed, using data from 47 studies in 30 countries, that the longer a woman breast-feeds, the *less* likely she is to develop breast cancer. The effect was highly significant, and the lower rates and shorter periods of breast-feeding typical of developed countries make "a major contribution to the high incidence of breast cancer" in such nations. Another example: mothers who nurse during the first year are strongly protected against depression. Nearly ten percent of new mothers suffer depression within six months of their child's birth, and breast-feeding cuts the chance of depression in half, according to a 2002 study by psychologist Elizabeth Mezzacappa of the Columbia College of Physicians and Surgeons in New York.[18]

It is worth mentioning that despite the benefits of breast-feeding, a warm and loving experience during bottle feeding may be preferable to being breast-fed by a tense or overly neurotic mother. Mothers who cannot or wish not to breast-feed are not necessarily harming their babies; love and the sense of connection *can* be fostered even without breast-feeding, just as emotional damage can be inflicted on a breast-feeding infant by neurotic parents.

– 7 –

Even Before Birth

A large body of evidence shows (as we have already seen) that even pre-birth experience can have major and lifelong effects.[19]

It has become well known, for instance, that poor nutrition can adversely affect the fetus. Without adequate folic acid (a B vitamin), pregnant mothers greatly increase their babies' risk of neural tube defects, including spina bifida. Drugs and other substances can also permanently alter the development of a child in utero; Thalidomide is the best-known example.

Harm to the fetus from a mother's smoking is also well-known.

Many studies have found that smoking during pregnancy increases the risk of problems for the child, ranging from hyperactivity to learning difficulties and worse. A recent Swedish study of 17,000 children found that those born to mothers who smoked—even to those who smoked fewer than 10 cigarettes per day—had more than *four times* the risk of developing diabetes later in life.[20] How could smoking *by the mother* cause diabetes *later in the life of her children?* Because, apparently, "smoking deprives the fetus of nutrients, resulting in lifelong metabolic abnormalities."

Still, a large number of pregnant women continue to smoke. A study in 1995 by Brigham and Women's Hospital in Boston found that between 18 and 19 percent of pregnant women smoke, and that the results are horrifying, including 5,600 infant deaths. In addition, smoking by pregnant mothers results in roughly 115,000 miscarriages, over 50,000 low-birthweight babies, and about 22,000 babies needing intensive care—each year, in the United States alone.[21]

Other drugs have adverse effects as well, of course. A pregnant mother's use of alcohol, methamphetamine, or cocaine can cause serious and often lifelong problems for the fetus. These aren't the only substances that can cause problems, as most of us know.

What fewer know is that it doesn't take a mother's drug addiction or serious malnutrition to cause lifelong problems for the newborn. Simple stress can have major, long-term effects.

Furthermore, early experience affects more than physical development. It affects character, behavior, and future experience itself.

For example, researchers at the University of Wisconsin's Harlow Primate Laboratory found that surprisingly low levels of stress in pregnant rhesus monkeys produced large effects in their offspring. One stressor in the experiment was "(t)hree noise bursts…randomly sounded over a 10-minute period." The offspring of these monkeys were visibly fearful and anxious compared to normal offspring from unstressed mothers. The offspring of the stressed mothers were also "slower to learn, more shy, clumsier, had less effective immune systems, and weighed less" than the offspring of unstressed mothers.[22]

– 8 –

NEGATIVE EVENTS early in life have negative consequences. A *lack* of such events *improves* the chance for a positive outcome.

The point is that what the studies are telling us can be phrased in different ways. To say that early neglect causes later problems, for example, is to also say that reducing early neglect improves the average outcome for a given group of infants or children.

If the combination of a birth complication and rejection by the mother makes a male infant three times more likely to exhibit violent behavior later in life (as one 30-year study found),[23] then the study means that male children will have a lower statistical risk of showing later violent behavior *if the infants have good births and loving mothers.* Society-wide, reducing such risk factors would have major benefits: the study's authors estimate as much as 18 percent of *all* violent crime is related to these two specific factors, for example.

Every study showing negative results of trauma is also showing the *positive* results of loving, non-traumatic care. Trauma and pain early in life create misery and a higher chance for violence later in life. In contrast, love and other proper care early on set the stage for a loving and healthy life in adulthood.

– 9 –

SCIENTIFIC EVIDENCE shows ever more clearly that early experience sets the tone and character for later experience, and that each person's life is powerfully affected by events from childhood, infancy, and even before. Sensitive dependence on early conditions it is a fundamental truth about complex, iterative systems generally.

In short, "the child is father to the man."

– 10 –

TAKING "SENSITIVE DEPENDENCE on early conditions" seriously is the only way to solve the problems so apparent in the human condition. Absolutely nothing will replace the need to treat pregnant mothers, newborns, infants, and children with compassion and love and respect.

When enough newcomers to this green and lovely Earth *are* treated with compassion, love, and respect, the human world will *become* more compassionate and loving and respectful of each human being.

The computer industry has a term: GIGO, meaning "garbage in, garbage out." That is what we've had in large parts of the world until now: garbage as input, in the form of mistreatment of the young, leading to garbage as output, in the form of crime, war, tyranny, emotional damage, etc., in the world at large.

The fix is simple: stop using garbage for input. In human terms, we need to move towards CICO—"compassion in, compassion out."

Love begets love; pain begets pain. Take your pick.

Chapter 6

LOVE AND FREEDOM:
THE FUNDAMENTALS
OF PARADISE

To love is to receive a glimpse of heaven.   — *Karen Sunde*

I was not born to be forced. I will breathe after my own fashion.
     — *Henry David Thoreau*

Love includes freedom. Indeed, denying freedom to someone is the opposite of loving them; murder, slavery and kidnapping are extreme examples, but *any* use of initiated coercion harms love.

Love and freedom may also be seen as two sides of a human duality, much like yin and yang. Emphasizing one over the other causes problems because an imbalance means that at least one side is below the healthy, optimal level. High levels of both love and freedom are necessary for a healthy society.

We require love because we are all *one*. We are all connected. We are all brothers and sisters, and love is what we were born for.

63

Yet we also require *freedom* because each of us is a separate and unique individual. We have our own thoughts and talents, our own preferences and desires. This natural diversity among individuals brings strength to the group.

As an individual, your uniqueness makes you who you are. When that uniqueness is denied, you feel disrespected; being part of the whole is not the same as being a cog in a machine. Love includes *both* a sense of oneness with others *and* respect for each person as a unique, free, and self-controlling individual.

Prosperity is an inevitable, although not instantaneous, side-effect of a society characterized by love and freedom—because when people are emotionally healthy enough to know what they truly want, and when human energy is not hindered by coercive restrictions and centralized control, then human beings are able to satisfy human needs and desires with optimal efficiency. By "prosperity" I mean having real material needs comfortably met, not the neurotic quest for ever-more things regardless of need.

– 2 –

TREMENDOUS HARM is done by a lack of love and freedom, yet *seeing* this is difficult for many people. Recall what I said in the Preface: that *real change will require perceptual shifts of great magnitude.* Any paradigm change which threatens power structures or psychological defenses will meet resistance, no matter how accurate it is and no matter what the benefits are. People were once imprisoned or executed for suggesting that the Earth orbits the sun; a paradigm built around love and freedom is at *least* as threatening to the status quo and will inspire opposition on many levels.

This chapter looks at the connections between love and freedom, at some of the forces opposing love and freedom, and at the inevitable harm caused by their lack. Chapter Twelve discusses the benefits seen where love and freedom are at healthier levels.

– 3 –

Command is the growl of coercion crouching in ambush. Or we might aptly term it—violence in a latent state.
— *Herbert Spencer*

We ask you to renounce this old, weary, hopeless way of force, ever tearstained and bloodstained, which has gone on so long under emperors and autocrats and governing classes . . .
— *Auberon Herbert, "A Plea for Voluntaryism", 1908*

WHEN LEVELS of love and freedom are low, disaster is certain. Examples are everywhere. Often it happens that a group emphasizes one side of the duality at expense of the other. For instance, early America focused on freedom at the expense of love; Marxism focuses on love at the expense of freedom. As a result, neither is a good example of *either* love or freedom. Kill love in a society and you destroy freedom; diminish freedom and you drive a stake through love's heart.

Consider two well-known flaws of the early United States. First, slavery was allowed in some of the states. Second, American Indians were sometimes mass-murdered, their land was stolen, and the survivors were forced onto reservations.

In both cases, *the target groups were not being treated with love or compassion.*

It is equally clear that in both cases, *freedom was being denied* to the target group.

One cannot enslave or murder someone while treating them with compassion. Loving someone requires and includes allowing them the rights of life, liberty, and property.

– 4 –

TO SEE HOW REPUGNANT initiated coercion really is, consider that if you add coercion to sex, it becomes rape. Nothing else is necessary for sex to become rape; the addition of coercion is *all it takes*.

Gandhi pointed out that one who uses coercion "is guilty of deliberate violence," and anyone who has been the victim of coercion would surely agree. It is no surprise, then, that "coercion" is listed in the criminal code as a serious crime in at least some of the United States. Most real crimes (as opposed to infractions of arbitrary political restrictions, prohibitions, and requirements) *are* crimes *because* they involve the use of coercion.

Now consider a profound and disquieting fact: *governments are tools for the use of initiated coercion across entire societies.* This, despite wide acknowledgment that initiated coercion turns *anything* into something vile.

Coercion may be needed in self-defense, and when dealing with murderers and others who use *initiated* coercion—and this is where the State gets its license to coerce, at least in most people's minds. But is coercion necessary in *everything* a government does? Is *initiating* coercion against peaceful human beings even decent or reasonable?

– 5 –

MARXISM'S EMPHASIS on compassion at the expense of freedom brought even worse results than from the opposite focus in early America. The "compassion" was to be supplied (at gunpoint if necessary, of course) by the State. Pure Marxism—see The Communist Manifesto by Marx and Engels—is Communism, and Communism has been the worst man-made disaster in history.

That is no overstatement. The authors—Marxists themselves—of The Black Book of Communism: Crimes, Terror, Repression (858 pages, *Harvard University Press*, 1999) estimate that Communist governments murdered between eighty-five million and one hundred million people in the twentieth century. Even the smaller figure comes to roughly one million murders per year, starting with the Russian Revolution in 1917. The authors go on to describe this as "the most colossal case of political carnage in history."

Indeed, the book's Foreword is titled "The Uses of Atrocity"; its

Introduction is titled "The Crimes of Communism." Stalin, for one example, murdered millions of Ukrainians in 1932–1933* by simply confiscating the food they grew and selling it abroad for hard currency. Peasants in the Ukraine who were found with stored food were typically executed on the spot.

– 6 –

The Black Book is not the only source one might check to confirm the incredible danger to love—and to life itself—created by a lack of freedom (i.e., by coercive government power). Professor R. J. Rummel, perhaps the world's foremost authority on government murder, recently upgraded his estimate of government murder (including governments of all types) for the twentieth century to 262,000,000. That is approximately *six times the number killed in all the wars of the twentieth century*, including World War I and World War II. Two hundred sixty-two million is also twice the number of government murders Rummel could find in all of pre-twentieth-century history (Death by Government, *Transaction Publishers*, 1994).

Here is what Rummel has to say about awareness of these stunning facts, even among academics in related fields:

> *I think the ignorance of the incredible murder by government is a moral, intellectual, and academic scandal. It is the biggest and most significant black hole in our educational system and literature.*[24]

Rummel maintains a website with several thousand pages of documentation on this topic at *http://www.hawaii.edu/powerkills/welcome.html*.

The lesson here is that without freedom, love is in danger—

---

* The Black Book reports that "more than six million" died in the famine (page 159). Another source, The U.S. Library of Congress, gives the estimate of "six to seven million" dead; Revelations from the Russian Archives: Ukrainian Famine *http://www.loc.gov/exhibits/archives/ukra.html*

even when love is the supposed reason for restricting freedom in the first place. Love does not long survive without freedom, any more than human beings survive without food or air.

– 7 –

WHAT OF SOCIALISM? Must it be linked to government coercion? Of course not. Marx himself said that the Communist state would eventually "wither away." Socialism would remain, but the coercive state would not. Marx was not the only one to make such an assertion:

> *All Socialists are agreed that the political state, and with it political authority, will disappear as a result of the coming social revolution. . .*
> — *Frederick Engels, "On Authority" 1872*

> *While the State exists, there can be no freedom. When there is freedom there will be no State.*
> — *Lenin, "State and Revolution", 1919*

Indeed, the idea that government-enforced, coercive, total socialism (i.e., Communism) would eventually lead to a society *without* State coercion was fundamental to Marxist theory. Violent revolution and then government coercion (once Communists were in power) were thought necessary to begin the process of freeing the masses from control by those with economic power, but the ultimate goal was a world of compassion and brotherhood—*without* government coercion.

Of course, using force and violence to create a world of love and compassion is insane. The use of coercion is exactly what betrayed Marx's powerful, haunting vision (poorly imagined though it was) of a healthier, more loving world. The compassionate socialist utopia envisioned by Marxists became a nightmare of tyranny, famine, and epic mass-murder. I cannot think of a more powerful example of why the end does not justify the means.

Despite the cautionary examples of Communism and of other

attempts to create a better world via coercion, most nations today—even those not usually considered "socialist"—mix coercive socialism with some degree of freedom for the markets and for personal life. I see two main reasons for this:

A) The promise of a compassionate, loving world is attractive enough to inspire fealty and passion in the masses—despite the promise being visibly false when implemented by government power. That same use of coercion actually strengthens the appeal, because it includes the forced transfer of wealth *from* the more productive *to* the less productive. In short, coercive socialism's appeal combines the universal longing for a compassionate world with simple greed and resentment.

B) This mass appeal makes coercive socialism a better tool for those in power than the "divine right of kings" and other frameworks previously used to control the masses.

I use the term "coercive socialism" to differentiate socialism imposed by a government from *non-coercive* forms of socialism, such as communes, families, churches, service groups, and other socially-oriented groups and organizations that do *not* use initiated coercion and violence. This is a critical distinction. "*Socialism*" and "*coercive socialism*" are entirely different in character and result.

To the extent that freedom prevails in coercive-socialist nations, the results are tolerable if not optimal. To the extent that *coercion* prevails, the results are negative: corruption, erosion of wealth, and often far worse, as with the forced sterilization of "those not worthy of having children" in Sweden, where over 60,000 men and women were sterilized against their will from 1934 to 1974.* One extreme example of socialist coercion (caused in

---

* *Washington Post*, August 29, 1997, p. A1.

part by the extremes of emotional damage in both the government "leaders" and in the population at large) is, of course, National Socialism in Germany under Adolph Hitler.

"Nazi" is a (partially phonetic) contraction of the German for "National Socialist" and yes, Hitler's Germany was indeed a "third-way" socialist nation, with anti-smoking campaigns, make-work programs, coercive regulation of business for the public good, and other programs of social concern. The National Socialists also insisted (as do socialist governments everywhere) on government control of—well, whatever those in power wanted control over. If National Socialism was bizarrely scattershot in its adoption and application of socialist theory, it was no further from the utopian Marxist ideal than all Communist nations and most socialist nations have been in practice. For example, putting all the means of production into the hands of the Communist state was *supposed* to lead to equality and compassion, *not* to a small group of socio-pathic rulers committing mass-murder and creating vast prison gulags, famine, and grinding poverty for the masses.

Any government is a nexus of coercive, corrupting power, and *that power is itself an abuse,* no matter what the alleged form of government. One of the dangers of coercive government socialism is that it provides an excuse for governments to gather even *more* power to themselves than they otherwise might.

Communist China has transitioned to a mix of coercive socialism and capitalism very similar to National Socialism—that is to say, the government no longer owns all the means of production, but of course it claims the "right" to regulate and control those means as well as anything else that government leaders *want* to control. The dramatic increase in economic freedom (compared to total government control of all production) has brought an equally dramatic increase in prosperity to a growing minority of the Chinese population.

Today's Chinese rulers have learned that if their nation is to generate wealth and power, it must have at least a measure of economic freedom. *Only* freedom allows for the broad creation of wealth that could make China an economic and military superpower. Depend on it: the desire for power, *not* any concern for the well-being of their subjects, is the reason China's leaders are allowing any economic freedom *at all* to Chinese citizens. Being left alone by one's government day-to-day (as most Chinese are) is certainly positive, but it is not the same as being free. When one's freedom or life can be cut short for talking about freedom or practicing one's religion,* one is simply a slave on a longer leash instead of a free human being.

– 8 –

IT IS WORTH REPEATING that *non-coercive* socialism is not a problem; the coercion, not the socialism, is what can turn a nation into a concentration camp. Start a commune or other socialist group if you want, but for heaven's sake don't use force and threats of force against the participants. Efficiency isn't the only value in life; socialism tends to be inefficient—especially in larger examples— but for a voluntary group this may not be an issue. If and as people become more emotionally healthy, I expect non-coercive socialism to become more common in a number of settings, but only time and experience will tell in detail what emotionally healthy people will make of their world.

One thing is certain: a healthy world will *not* use coercion as the foundation of society. The use of coercion is not only evil in and of itself: it also attracts (and helps to create) sociopaths. In turn, a sociopath with an army, a secret police force, and a national court system at his disposal can inflict far more damage than can

---

* A web search for **China + dissident + prison** or **"Falun Gong"** + **"organ harvesting"** will amply confirm this. One example: in March 2006, Ren Zhiyuan, a teacher from Shandong province, was sentenced to ten years in prison for posting an article titled "The Road to Democracy" ("Chinese Internet dissident gets 10-year sentence" by Sumner Lemon, IDG News Service, *http://www.pcworld. idg.com.au /pp.php?id=676551532&fp=2&fpid=1*).

an individual sociopath alone. That is the ultimate danger from *any* coercive government, and one sees this dynamic at work throughout history.

What type of person even *wants* coercive power over others in the first place? What type of person felt so desolate and powerless in childhood that *power* becomes an all-consuming need for them in adulthood? What type of person is motivated to do whatever is necessary to get *into* a position of power?

To say it as gently as possible: the type of person who *wants* (or is even willing to assume) coercive power over others is exactly the type of person who should never have it.

– 9 –

MONEY ISN'T EVERYTHING in life, but it isn't *nothing*, either. For that reason, it is important to understand that coercive socialism erodes prosperity. This erosion of wealth is inevitable, and of course non-socialist government coercion *also* erodes prosperity; it is the coercion, not the socialism, that causes most of the problem. But government socialism, by its very nature, includes large doses of coercion and directs much of that coercion straight at economic activity. More of life is typically controlled by force and threats of force, and more of one's income is taken by the state in a socialist nation. Combined with the perverse incentives of *reward for non-productivity* and *penalties for being productive*, this coercion chips away at a nation's wealth.

In the real world, not a single poor nation has ever changed to a coercive-socialist form of government and then found prosperity. Plenty of well-off nations have gone the other way, however (including the poster-child for coercive socialism, Sweden, which ranked third among industrial nations for income per capita in 1970 and now ranks considerably lower), and it isn't necessary for the words "socialist" or "Marxist" to be used in any official capacity for this to happen. Argentina is an example of a once-wealthy nation ("Rich as an Argentine" was a common saying in the early to mid-1900s) driven to the poorhouse in large part by well-meaning social programs and other coercive-socialist policy despite not calling itself socialist. In Africa, coercive socialism has been a factor in keeping much of the continent impoverished and tyrannized, while elsewhere, nations with no natural resource wealth to speak of—Hong Kong under the British and Switzerland, for two examples—have become wealthy by eschewing coercive socialism in favor of strong human rights (freedom) and weak, highly *restrained* governments.

Freedom puts power in the hands of the people instead of in the hands of government bureaucrats, politicians, and the behind-the-scenes power elite. Freedom allows people to create prosperity; Marxism, like other forms of un-freedom, impedes the creation of prosperity and erodes whatever prosperity already exists, eventually concentrating wealth in the hands of a shrinking group of oligarchs and their cronies. This process can take decades, but it happens nonetheless and without fail.

Despite that, Marxist thinking continues to hold mind-share in nations around the world, and I would argue that the influence of this failed, coercive system is greater than ever. Much of the politics even in modern-day America is simply coercive socialism in disguise; *any* form of central government charity or regulation or other "compassionate" meddling that is paid for with coercive taxation is more Marxist than not.

Charity and regulation are important, but *coercion* in applying or paying for such policies does what coercion *always* does: turns whatever it touches into an unhealthy and corrupt imitation of the real thing.

The Red Cross and Underwriters Laboratories* are examples of free-market responses to charity and regulation, respectively.

---

* Underwriters Laboratories is a non-government, non-profit safety testing and certifying organization. Founded more than a century ago in 1894, UL is the largest and best-known safety testing organization in the world. You almost certainly have items in your home that are "UL listed."

Neither requires your support at gunpoint. For that very reason, both have *reasons* to provide customer satisfaction. Both organizations are far more efficient and infinitely less likely to cause harm or to become corrupt than are governments. Neither the Red Cross nor Underwriter's Labs has ever "lost track" of over $1 trillion, as has the Pentagon in just the last few years.* Neither the Red Cross nor Underwriter's Labs is a danger to you or to anyone else.

In contrast, the Food and Drug Administration has allowed the American pharmaceutical industry to become one of the top causes of death in the United States; several studies in recent years have found that over 100,000 Americans are dying annually from FDA- •
approved prescription drugs. At the same time, drug prices have skyrocketed beyond many people's ability to pay. For that matter, medical mistakes (in the government-regulated and government-licensed medical industry) also cause approximately 100,000 deaths per year in the United States.**

Instead of more deaths and higher prices, free-market regulation of the vitamin and supplement industry has produced both a *lower* trend for prices and far *safer* products than the pharmaceutical industry offers. This is typical of market regulation; the computer hardware and software industries are other examples, as are consumer electronics and communications. "Cheaper and better" is exactly what one *expects* of the marketplace; "expensive, corrupt, and dangerous" is what one typically gets from coercive regulation or from outright government takeover of almost anything.

Dangerous products and staggering prices are not even the worst of it, however. Governments, as you will recall, are enablers and agents of the worst crimes imaginable. Unlike businesses and

---

* "Military waste under fire: $1 trillion missing—Bush plan targets Pentagon accounting" by Tom Abate, Chronicle Staff Writer, *San Francisco Chronicle*, Sunday, May 18, 2003, page A-1

** See, for example, Dr. Joseph Mercola's well-researched and heavily footnoted "Death by Medicine, Part I" at *http://www.mercola.com/2003/nov/26/death_by_medicine.htm*.

other non-coercive groups, many governments amass nuclear arsenals, start wars, incinerate cities, poison children and adults with depleted uranium, and stockpile chemical and biological weapons. Death camps and gulags are *not* what one gets from Microsoft or the Salvation Army; they are government programs, without exception. Businesses and other non-coercive organizations do not imprison or execute people who oppose them. Nor do non-government organizations hunt down and imprison people for peacefully using alcohol or marijuana or other drugs.

It is no overstatement to say that *any new product as dangerous as coercive government would quickly be banned.* It is time, and long past time, to consider a less dangerous and less corrupt method for organizing society.

– 10 –

IF LOVE FOR OTHERS requires letting them be free, it is equally true that **freedom *in human affairs* requires love**. Because people often see "freedom" as merely a lack of coercive interference, it is easy to miss the human element here. But we are *human* beings, not inanimate objects. For instance, a pebble on the beach may be "free" but that has no more meaning for a pebble than does any other physical condition. "Meaning" in the human sense involves either *feeling* or *abstract reasoning*, or both. Pebbles and other inanimate objects have neither.

One clear example of how freedom dies without love is Germany under Hitler. Typical child-rearing practices in Germany had, for many decades, been cruel, harsh, and designed to enforce obedience to authority. In short, freedom was largely displaced by authoritarianism, compassion by emotional coldness, and love by seething hatred. This hatred was eventually channeled towards Jews and other minorities. In essays, articles, and especially in her book For Your Own Good: Hidden cruelty in child-rearing and the roots of violence, Alice Miller provides a heart-rending look at how children—including Hitler himself—were treated in Germany

during the nineteenth and early twentieth century. It is not difficult to understand how the horrors of the Hitler years could have
happened, considering the horrors inflicted upon so many
Germans during childhood.

When I say that "freedom requires love" I am not just being
poetic. Without a reasonable level of emotional health in society,
freedom fails and real horrors become all too possible. Love, compassion and respect during infancy and childhood are basic
requirements for a healthy adulthood. Too many unhealthy adults
in a nation make for a dangerous situation, no matter what type of
government is in place.

– *11* –

THE MARKET PROVIDES another lesson in why freedom requires love.
As *human* beings, we are more than brothers and sisters: we depend
upon each other to create the human world we live in; we depend
upon others for our very survival. When people serve others without the use of coercion, we call the result either "charity" (when the
effort is provided without monetary compensation) or "the marketplace" (when people are creating income for themselves and
their families by providing goods or services to others). Both charity and market activity show love at work, because the participants
are treating others with respect and *without* coercion.

A look at the real world shows how critically important voluntary cooperation in the market really is. See, for instance, the
well-known essay "I, Pencil" by Leonard E. Read.* Thousands of
people around the world, with many different skills, are needed to
create even a simple wooden pencil. How many does it take to create
an automobile? To grow and transport the food that reaches your
table? To create the machines, find and transport and refine the fuel,
and do everything else that makes such miracles possible? How many

---

* There is more detail here than most would imagine. Consider reading Leonard
  Read's essay, posted at several places on the web including *http://209.217.49.*
  168/vnews.php?nid=316

people does it take to create the media content that enriches your life? The vast, complex, finely coordinated and *voluntary* web of interaction that continually creates our world is staggering, and *only functions because it is a voluntary and emergent system*. Trying to turn this miracle into something that is centrally-planned, centrally-controlled, and coercively-run is a mistake of the greatest magnitude.

Consider a single broad area of the marketplace; reflect for a moment on all that has gone into creating the hardware, the standards, and the content of the internet, of television, of motion pictures—such as the 910 people and 70,441 man-hours it took to create a 49-second sequence in *Star Wars Episode III* *—and of books, magazines, newspapers, and games.

The market brings all this together peacefully and voluntarily. Coercive government, in contrast, simply wrecks this natural and effective social machinery, as we see in those areas increasingly controlled by government, such as pharmaceuticals and medicine.

– *12* –

HENRY DAVID THOREAU understood the connection between love and freedom, and in *Civil Disobedience* he states the truth plainly: "*That government is best which governs not at all.*"** Why would that be true? Because government is simply coercion, and *reducing coercion to the minimum* is the only approach compatible with a loving, healthy world. Love, freedom, and prosperity are all endangered and eroded by the widespread use of coercive power.

Oxford professor and author J.R.R. Tolkien held a similar view,

---

* The DVD of this film contains a feature-length extra that covers the process in great detail including interviews with many of the people involved. *The San Diego Union-Tribune* carried a story on this topic, which may still be on-line at *http:// www.signonsandiego.com/news/features/homevideo/20051031-9999_dvd 162.html*

** *Civil Disobedience* was a major influence on Gandhi and Martin Luther King. The essay is on the web at, among other places, *http://eserver.org/thoreau/civil. html*. There is dispute over the similar Jefferson quotation ("That government is best which governs least"); it is not known to appear in any of Jefferson's writings, although it certainly fits with his beliefs as expressed throughout his life.

and his <u>Lord of the Rings</u> trilogy is built around the idea that the "Ring of Power" must be destroyed rather than given to the "right" person. The Ring clearly represents coercive state power, and the corrupting influence of this power is a major thread in the LOTR storyline.

To my knowledge, Tolkien himself never said that the Ring was meant as a metaphor, but the characteristics of the Ring—its "great and terrible power" including the ability it gives to dominate entire regions, the relentless corruption it causes in anyone who holds the Ring, the fact that even good intentions are turned into evil results by the Ring's use, the near-universal (and nearly insane) refusal of people to part with the Ring once they have it—are a perfect match for coercive government power. Other metaphors have been proposed, but none fit the characteristics Tolkien ascribed to the Ring nearly as well.

In Tolkien's Middle-Earth as in real life, coercive power is evil, and using it with even the best of intentions can only bring disaster. Frodo is the hero of the trilogy because he alone is immune—mostly, at any rate—to the siren call of the Ring's evil power. Even Gandalf, the ancient, wise, and powerful wizard of the tale, is conflicted and terrified at the prospect of even touching the Ring. When Frodo attempts to hand the Ring to Gandalf, the wizard recoils, explaining that he would only use the Ring from a desire to do good, but would instead unleash "a power too great and terrible to imagine." He tells Frodo to never offer him the Ring again.

One *cannot* do good with the evil of coercive power—that is the message of <u>Lord of the Rings</u>. An honest look at history shows Gandalf's concern to be more realistic than any of us might wish.

Does it not make sense to at least consider whether this agency of war, genocide, poverty, misery, and tyranny is *positive*—or even tolerable? Does it not make sense to ask whether an institution run entirely on the basis of coercion is really a *necessary* evil?

Might it instead be merely an *ancient* evil?

– 13 –

MY SIMPLE PRESCRIPTION for the problem of coercive government, and my only political viewpoint, is: "Take the coercion out."

Removing initiated coercion from government automatically
removes most of the direct evil which governments are guilty of
and allows the positive things government does (real, fundamen-
tally non-coercive functions that governments have taken over,
such as road maintenance and air traffic control) to continue—
with more efficiency, higher quality, lower cost, and less corruption.
When funded and carried out without coercion, such functions are
exposed to market forces (competition, in particular) that insure
respect for customers—at least among firms that wish to stay in
business. Removing the "right" of governments to initiate coercion
also removes the coercive *power* that corporations now purchase
for their own benefit—via expensive lobbying and other methods—including corporate welfare and the "industrial" side of
America's military-industrial complex. The worst corporate behavior is both encouraged and *enabled* by government coercion.

> *It is a mistake to assume that government must necessarily last for-
> ever. The institution marks a certain stage of civilization—is
> natural to a particular phase of human development. It is not
> essential, but incidental. As amongst the Bushmen we find a state
> antecedent to government, so may there be one in which it shall
> have become extinct.*
>
> — Herbert Spencer

– 14 –

Chapter Summary

LOVE AND FREEDOM are two sides of a duality in human life, and
when that duality is out of balance, bad things happen. Neither love
nor freedom long survives without the other.

Creating widespread prosperity from scratch is incredibly
hard work, and long before the job was finished, Marxist and other
coercive-socialist ideologies dishonestly *cornered the franchise* on

"compassion" in politics. These ideologies are based upon an error: that positive reinforcement (reward) for non-productivity combined with aversive conditioning (penalties) for production of wealth will create a prosperous and compassionate society. There is an even more dire error embedded in this scheme—that using initiated coercion to achieve our goals is right and proper.

These errors are perfect tools for the ruling class. George Bernard Shaw put it succinctly: *"A government that robs Peter to pay Paul can always depend on the support of Paul."*

Today's power elite gravitate to coercive-socialist forms of government for exactly that reason: coercive socialism works for them as a tool for misleading and controlling the masses. Coercive socialism also wrecks entire nations and harms the people it claims to help, but that is not an issue for the elite.

It must be an issue for us, however, and we must help make it an issue for the public at large. For that to happen, the public must begin to understand the fundamentals. If the public ever *does* understand these fundamentals, the movement towards Paradise will be unstoppable.

Love without freedom is a fraud; freedom without love is *also* a fraud. In both cases the situation is unbalanced and unstable, and the result—if the imbalance is severe—is always a nightmare.

More than balance is needed, of course: high levels of both love and freedom are necessary for a healthy, compassionate, and prosperous world. Such a world will not come into being at gunpoint, or by means of coercive politics. The most important tools we have for creating such a world are better treatment of infants and children, and careful, truthful use of language. In particular, we must spread awareness of the evil nature and dire results of initiated coercion, and highlight the positive results of freedom and love. This must include frequent description of concrete, real-world examples, as covered in Chapter Twelve.

One further point: *Twenty-first century technology will make this a life and death issue for mankind.* Future technology will greatly empower either freedom or tyranny, as it will also empower either compassion or cold-heartedness.

The road ahead branches sharply, and our legacy will be one or the other: a world of tyranny and pain, or a very *different* world—the world of our hearts, the world for which every new human life is born.

CHAPTER 7

THE HUMAN CONDITION
DRAMATIZED

Fiction reveals truth that reality obscures.
— *Ralph Waldo Emerson*

WE SEE THE IMPORTANCE OF CHANGE only by facing the human condition squarely, but our defenses make this difficult. Defending against painful subjects is, after all, what defenses are *for*.

For the most part, this chapter approaches the topic from the perspective of popular horror fiction—a literary form with more insight than usually given credit for.

– 2 –

OTHER GENRES ALSO dramatize the human condition, of course: even a story about aliens must say something, however obliquely, about human nature if the author wishes to engage the reader's interest. Comedy, romance, drama, and other genres can all tell us

83

much about what it means to be human. Importantly, fiction often shows us healthy and positive human character and behavior. Warm family relationships, courage in the face of adversity or tyranny, openness to feeling, integrity, honesty, or simple compassion can be found in almost any genre, even if (as is often the case) set against backdrops of violence, corruption, or other symptoms of emotional damage. Schindler's List is a well-known example (both the Thomas Keneally book and Steven Spielberg's film) in which a seemingly callous businessman finds that his own sense of compassion is drawing him to save Jews from the Nazis, despite the very real danger of being imprisoned or executed for such "crime."

For children and adults who may have had few positive role models (or none), fiction can introduce and reinforce the possibility of a healthier life. For instance, in the Nancy Meyers film Something's Gotta Give, Diane Keaton plays a woman (Erica Barry) who suffers a breakup; she reacts by experiencing her grief over a period of months instead of pushing it down or denying it. We see Barry, a playwright, bursting into tears while at her desk writing; coming awake in bed with a start, crying; sitting at the beach in front of her house crying, and so on. Without lingering uncomfortably on these episodes, the film shows us a character allowing herself to feel deeply about a traumatic event, over time and for as long as necessary. Further, we see that this is positive for Barry; instead of suffering endlessly and going cold or brittle emotionally, she feels the *good* in her life as deeply as the bad, and stays warm and strong as a person while gradually freeing herself from the trauma of the breakup. The screenplay (also by Meyers) and Keaton's acting do a terrific job of making Barry's openness to feeling seem natural, healthy, and real.

Millions of people grow up not even knowing that such a thing is possible—that one can feel deeply about painful events, and about life generally, instead of pushing feelings down and trying to forget they exist. For someone in a family where crying "just isn't done," a film like <u>Something's Gotta Give</u> can be a powerful glimpse into a healthier, more meaningful, and more *human* way to live.

Many other films (and books, plays, short stories, and even television episodes) show positive human behavior and relationships. I believe such material has a very real and healthy effect in the world.

Of course, it is also important to see and understand the *unhealthy* aspects of the current human condition (as a motivation for change, if nothing else), and that is where horror fiction excels. This will be our focus for the remainder of the chapter.

– 3 –

IT IS NOT A NEW OBSERVATION that people are emotionally damaged. In the 1880s, Friedrich Nietzsche made the point poetically yet bluntly, writing, "I fear that the animals consider man as a being like themselves that has lost in a most dangerous way its sound animal common sense; they consider him the insane animal, the laughing animal, the weeping animal, the miserable animal." [25]

Not surprisingly, the most effective and popular horror fiction parallels reality by dramatizing this emotional damage. The truth is softened in these stories by use of details that are clearly fictitious, while certain oft-denied human fundamentals are retained. It is this blatant near-description of denied reality that gives the best horror stories their power, scope, and impact.

Common horror-story elements are nearly transparent in this regard. For example:

    ○ **The loss of innocence, and** (more severe) **the loss of the real self.** One or both of these elements is at the root of every horror tale involving ordinary people who are transformed into something evil, as opposed to stories of monsters, aliens, or other non-human beings who prey upon, but do not transform, human victims.

○ **The survival of the** (now-suppressed) **real self,** which is often described as buried but not destroyed. In vampire tales, for example, the vampires—recently made ones, especially—may become their real selves again after their "master" is killed, or, briefly, after being mortally wounded. In tales of possession (e.g., The Exorcist) this aspect is a given; the person possessed returns to his or her "normal" self after the demon is driven out.

○ **The replacement of the victim's natural feeling and compassion,** at least to some extent, **with corruption and cold-bloodedness.**

○ **The hidden nature of the loss;** the victim can often pass for "normal." This helps him or her prey upon new victims more effectively. It also isolates the victim; the tragedy may not be seen by family and friends, preventing them from offering help or sympathy to the victim. In some stories, such as werewolf tales, the victims behave (and experience life) normally at some times, but are overcome by the evil within them at other times. In other stories, the afflicted are "putting on an act" when appearing normal; they are being calculating, and are not genuine in their emotions.

○ **The hidden nature of the evil itself;** it is pervasive, but unseen. Hiding from whatever is afflicting people is almost impossible; it is everywhere, yet one usually cannot point to it. Those who warn others of the danger are often viewed as deluded or insane.

○ **The infectious nature of the loss:** the damned infect others.

○ **The evil is often described as *ancient*,** carried down across long spans of time.

Not all of those elements appear in every horror story, of course. But a majority are found in a wide range of horror fiction, old and new—for good reason:

They are exactly true of the real horror story we call "the human condition."

– *4* –

A few examples of horror stories that fit this chapter's premise:

○ **Vampires,** from Bram Stoker's original <u>Dracula</u> to John Carpenter's 1998 <u>Vampires</u>, and even newer films and novels; more are produced every year

○ **Werewolves,** from medieval folk tales to recent versions of the same theme, such as the 1999 film <u>American Werewolf in Paris</u>; again, the popularity of this genre is on-going, and some stories, such as the 2003 film <u>Underworld</u>, contain *both* werewolf and vampire characters

○ <u>The Exorcist</u> and other tales of **possession**

These are stories in which the victims are infected or changed by evil, but in which they may retain their real selves. The real self becomes buried but is not destroyed. Recovering the self may be possible, although in some stories, only for a few moments at the time of death.

Another group of stories involves victims who are physically replaced, either mechanically or by an invading organism, yet appear normal, such as:

○ <u>The Stepford Wives</u> (less so, the 2004 remake)

○ <u>The Thing</u> (the 1950s original and the 1980s remake)

    ○ <u>Invasion of the Body Snatchers</u> (again, the original and the
      remake)

In these tales, the real self is destroyed and not recoverable, yet
the person appears normal—at least, normal enough to fool most
of the people, most of the time (to paraphrase Abe Lincoln's
famous observation about politicians).

Few people would have trouble adding to these lists. To an extent,
even <u>Alien</u> fits the template, although it is mainly a creature film.

Most creature films are clearly not among the two groups we
are discussing. <u>Jaws</u> is a good example: in <u>Jaws</u>, a great white shark
kills people. The only transformation the victims go through is into
fishfood, and when they're dead, they're gone.

$$- \; 5 \; -$$

HORROR FICTION can be extremely effective at generating emotional response. The reason should be obvious: we may not live
among vampires, but we do, all of us, live in a world where most
people have lost their souls—their real selves.

We live in a world where so *many* have lost their souls that
mass murder has been repeatedly conceived and carried out in
nations large and small; a world where crime and child abuse and
other cruelties are common; a world where people are so miserable that they spend enough money on illegal drugs to make
billionaires out of "drug lords"—while risking prison or worse in
the process. Legal drugs are often more damaging than the illegal
ones, yet they too are consumed at stunning rates in nearly all
nations. Tobacco, for instance, remains a huge business despite
warnings on the packaging plainly stating that the product may
cause, among other problems, death from cancer, heart disease, or
emphysema.

We may not fear being bitten by a vampire or becoming
"undead," but as children, we grew up in this world, and I am convinced that at some level we knew of its sickness, whether we lived

directly in the worst of it or not. Furthermore, most of us suffered enough early trauma that repression of old experience became an on going, real-life curse.

That same repression prevents full experience of events and feelings in the present, for a variety of reasons. It literally makes us "unfeeling," to whatever extent we are afflicted. This repression, and the painful feelings being repressed, are the driving force behind neurotic symptoms of all types, from hypersexuality to heavy drug use, from domestic violence to racism. People are unique in their past experience and in the precise structure of their defenses, but the engine driving it all—driving nearly every-thing other than healthy, natural behavior—is deprivation and pain from early in life.*

I believe that most children are aware, at some level, that this disaster has happened to the adults around them, that it is in the process of happening to other children they know, and that they, personally, are doomed to the same fate.

In short, most people's lives are ruined, in a manner and to an extent that few people—mercifully—are ever aware of. Like the vampires in Stephen King's 'Salem's Lot, this horror is everywhere, but it is difficult to see, to pinpoint, to talk about. Talking about it, in fact, generally brands someone as crazy. But to say it again: the state of the world, the daily news, the history books, and our own eyes and ears tell us the truth, if we care to listen.

Prevention—to reprise a theme—is the answer here. It is the *only* answer, long-term. The question is: are we too late?

Perhaps we are. We cannot know for certain in advance. It should make no difference in our actions, of course. Either way, we have only one sane option: to act as if there is time, yet, to save the world.

---

* See Appendices 1, 3, and 4 for support of this view.

CHAPTER 8

PREVENTION IS THE ONLY LONG-TERM SOLUTION

The Study makes it clear that time does not *heal some of the adverse experiences we found so common in the childhoods of a large population of middle-aged, middle class Americans. One does not 'just get over' some things, not even fifty years later.*

— *Vincent J. Felitti, MD, The Relationship of Adverse Childhood Experiences to Adult Health: Turning gold into lead, <u>Z psychsom Med Psychother</u>, 2002*

... violence and abuse pass from generation to generation as well as from one society to the next. Our stark conclusion is that we see the need to do much more to ensure that child abuse does not happen in the first place, because once these key brain alterations occur, there may be no going back.

— *Martin H. Teicher, "Scars That Won't Heal: The neurobiology of child abuse," <u>Scientific American</u>, March 2002*

A WORLD WITHOUT WIDESPREAD emotional damage will be a world unlike any we have seen. We will not live to see it in finished form, but we *can* begin the process of creating it.

How could we choose not to?

– 2 –

PREVENTION OF EMOTIONAL DAMAGE, on the widest possible scale, is the key requirement for building this new world. The reason is known to all of us: emotional damage from childhood never heals.[26]

That goes against every self-help book you have ever read, but it is true nonetheless. It is true despite there being an entire industry built around the idea that suffering adults can, by attending the right seminar, reading the right book, or learning the right attitude, *overcome* the damage that was done to them early in life.

To the extent that people benefit from such things, there is no reason to dissuade them from trying potential remedies. And some do benefit, in some ways, from earnest attempts to overcome early damage. Adult problems that stem from such damage can, in some cases, be resolved, or at least changed for the better.

But the uniformly high rates of recidivism for most neurotic symptoms tell us that something deeper and unchanging is driving those symptoms in the present. For example, alcoholics know that even after years of hard-earned sobriety, they are in danger of falling back into the habit of heavy drinking. This is a basic tenet of Alcoholics Anonymous,[27] for instance, and something I expect few social scientists would dispute, because the facts are quite clear. *Something* is driving the need that alcoholics have to "feel no pain," as a particularly insightful euphemism puts it.

– 3 –

IN SHORT, curing the sick is a noble goal, but it simply doesn't work where neurosis is concerned. Not to any great degree, at least. Not enough to make the sort of broad, society-wide changes that are needed.

Consider also that dictators, secret policemen, violent sociopaths, and others like them show no interest in "improving" themselves emotionally. Has *any* dictator ever sought therapy in hopes of becoming kinder and more decent? Has any warlord or crime boss done so?

Even if one did, would it help?

In the movie <u>Sleeper</u>, Woody Allen wakes up 200 years in the future; when he learns of how long he's been in cryosleep, he quips that had he been going to his therapist all that time, he might almost be cured by now. The joke works because the audience knows that psychotherapy, by and large, does not.

It isn't that patients never benefit from therapy, and of course there are many types of therapy to choose from. But the idea that, say, the sociopathic ruling class of Red China might have ever sought therapy, gotten well, and then decided to forgo the Tiananmen Square massacre or their murderous on-going persecution of Christians, Buddhists, Falun Gong, dissidents, and others is laughable—or would be, if so many murders and so much needless misery were not at issue.

It matters little, in the great scheme of things, that some forms of therapy are helpful to some people. Curing huge numbers of individuals of their emotional damage is simply not a realistic option. Neither is commanding or forcing them to behave as if they were healthy or compassionate; in most cases, force is likely to be counterproductive rather than merely useless.

– 4 –

To say that love cannot heal earlier damage is *not* to say it cannot, in many cases, prevent further damage. That is to say, love is still critical during childhood, and until and unless the child has become too damaged to benefit from love, he or she still needs and benefits from a loving relationship.

Later love does not negate earlier trauma but it can help reduce (rather than amplify) the on-going damage from that trauma. For example, one study of almost seven hundred infants, who were followed for thirty years, found that good child-rearing made a difference in those infants who had complications during and shortly after birth. Children who suffered both a birth complication and childhood trauma had about three times the health problems as the group average. Forming a close bond with at least one parent or caretaker gave these children better odds for long-term good health. [28]

– 5 –

TRADITIONALLY, we have looked to religion, philosophy, ethics, laws, and cultural norms to "civilize" men and women. This works to an extent, but history shows that it does not work well enough. We have too often seen that people can go to church regularly yet still commit violence, harbor racist feelings (or own slaves, for that matter), and exhibit any of the near-infinite array of neurotic symptoms, from internal tension and misery to serial murder. Attempts to control the behavior of adults who were emotionally damaged in childhood are simply not reliable, regardless of the approach and despite the good they often do.

Traditional methods of civilizing people are not consistent in their effects because early experience determines how each person will react to later influences. As Alice Miller has pointed out, the way someone is treated during infancy and early childhood not only has an effect upon that person's later experience and actions, but the message and the power of that early experience "will always be stronger than intellectual knowledge acquired at a later stage." [29] If the message is one of love, then as an adult, the person will have a strong foundation for a loving adulthood. If the message is one of anger, violence, indifference, or other negative treatment, then the person's adulthood will be affected in a negative manner.

Miller is talking especially about violent crime (including state-sanctioned violence, as with sadistic concentration camp guards), but of course the effects of early experience range all across the spectrum. *

Even a brief consideration of the forces involved in neurosis makes it clear that successfully improving the human condition, or even outward behavior, is beyond what we can reasonably expect from attempts to "improve" people after the damage has been done.

Imagine a child who has been mistreated from birth, and indeed since before birth: carried in the womb by a tense, neurotic mother, who was perhaps being abused by her husband, and who may have been a smoker, a drinker, a drug user. Then, after a cold, mechanistic (or otherwise traumatic) birth, the child grows up ignored, belittled, treated as a burden and a nuisance, or worse: as a punching bag, as a torture victim.

Will this child be relaxed, self-assured, generous, open, and loving? Will she feel good about herself, be trusting of others, and have empathy for those around her? Will he be gentle and concerned for those weaker or less fortunate than himself?

If not, will a weekend workshop on "self esteem" solve the problem? Will a self-help book put things right?

Of course not. Such things may or may not help the victim in some way, but they will certainly not eliminate the damage caused by years of daily insults, neglect, and other abuse. As studies have repeatedly shown, the trauma a person experiences in childhood remains, causing symptoms and misery, throughout life and right into old age.[30]

– 6 –

EARLY TRAUMA not only echoes throughout life, it can magnify later pains, as we saw in Chapter 5. Several studies have shown that traumatized infants experience hypersensitivity to later pain, possibly throughout life. They may be overwhelmed or traumatized by later events that they might have shrugged off had they not been traumatized earlier. It is worth noting here that each person's specific reaction to their own life experience is unique; for example, a *lower* reactivity to later pain and a flat affect generally are other possible after-effects of early trauma.

One need not be treated as horribly as described above to be damaged for life. One study found that children's own subjective assessment of how well-loved they *feel* correlates strongly with their later levels of health and happiness.[31] A family that looks picture-perfect from the outside may not, in fact, be a loving environment for the children.

We come into this world needing love more than anything else in the world; considering that a baby will literally die if it isn't cared for almost constantly for the first year or two, this need and the profound, desperate consciousness of it in the child are more than understandable. As a species, we would not have survived without them.

– 7 –

MORE LOVE, TENDERNESS, AND COMPASSION at the start of life create a more loving, tender, and compassionate adulthood—and a better, healthier life generally.

There is no substitute for this. It's love or nothing.

Fulfilling this genetic imperative does what nothing else—including later attempts to fix the damage—*can* do.

A truly healthy, free, and compassionate world will only emerge from a population that is *itself,* to a large extent, truly healthy, free, and compassionate.

Proper treatment right from the start—for *most* and eventually for *all* new members of the human family—is the primary ingredient needed to create a healthy, loving and compassionate world. This is what "sensitive dependence on early conditions" means in the human realm.

> *Feeling is what relating to anyone is all about. Children are just people. There are no special rules about relating to them that do not apply to any and all relationships. There's not much you have to do to children. You don't have to discipline them, lecture them, punish them, or lead them. All you have to do is talk to them, listen, hold them, be kind and free, spontaneous and easy and just let them be.*
> — *Arthur Janov,* The Feeling Child, *1973*

CHAPTER 9

WHAT IS LOVE?

We are all born for love. It is the principle of existence, and its only end.
— *Benjamin Disraeli*

There is, above all, a pervasive need to be loved. When we are children each new need in our development must be fulfilled in order for us to feel loved. Love is not something that rides above the satisfaction of needs, but something which is contained in such satisfaction.
— *Arthur Janov*

A man has not seen a thing who has not felt it.
— *Henry David Thoreau*

YEARS AGO I attended a talk by French obstetrician Frederick Leboyer. As part of the event he showed the film of a "Leboyer birth," including immersion in a bath of warm water after the birth. When the film was over, Leboyer took questions from the audience.

One doctor asked whether the bath might not be unsafe for the newborn; the water might get cold and the infant could be chilled.

97

This seemed odd, if only because Leboyer had delivered over a thousand babies and would surely have known if there had been problems with the water temperature. Besides, the water—and even the air in the room—was kept warm, to make the newborn as comfortable as possible.

Leboyer ignored such details and answered simply that if the questioner *felt* the bath was not right for a baby he was delivering, then he should not give the bath.

This answer fit perfectly with the theme of Dr. Leboyer's talk; while he had no quarrel with the need for modern medical technique where necessary, his focus was on getting parents, doctors, and nurses to consider the newborn's point of view. In turn, he believed this would lead to a more sensitive and compassionate approach, not in some mechanistic way but as part of a more sensitive outlook generally. It was this *sensitivity*, not any particular technique, that he was hoping to foster.

A compassionate sensitivity is the heart of love and is love's most powerful tool. Compassion makes love a guiding force more true and humane than detailed instructions or other artificial approaches can ever be.

– 2 –

WE HAVE BEEN talking about love throughout this book. It is time for a discussion and definition of the term.

In *Chapter One,* I said that:

> *The five-word sentence "Love can save the world" is a compressed version of the truth, and some of the missing detail is important.*

Love encompasses a very broad range of material; love implies compassion, concern for others, a willingness to let others live their own lives as they see fit, and many other things.

Love is not merely an intellectual concept; love exists on the level of feeling. A strictly intellectual understanding of love is thus a contradiction in terms.

For that reason, a definition of "love" requires both subjective and objective components.

1. A **subjective** definition: love as an internal event or set of feelings.

   The difficulty here is that transmitting this definition in *words* involves attempting to convey lower-level, non-verbal experience in higher-level, abstract language.

2. An **objective** definition: actions necessary to transmit the benefits of love to the object of affection; in particular, to a fetus, a newborn, an infant, or a child.

   The difficulty in this case is that "actions" include subtle and hard-to-quantify or even hard-to-detect variations in inner states; two people can act in ways that appear identical to a casual observer, but may project different messages by facial expression, body language, or in even more subtle ways. A repressed or otherwise largely-hidden emotional state (grief, fear, anger, etc.) may strongly impact the *recipient* without being quantifiable or even noticed by most other observers. Yet the tone of one's actions can be as important as the easily-visible part of the actions themselves, or even more so.

The Experience of Love

The subjective definition is one we all know, to the extent we **can** know, given our personal history and level of openness to feeling.

Still, it may be useful to pursue the definition further. The first definition of "love" (and the one which fits our discussion) in the American Heritage Dictionary of the English Language is:

A deep, tender, ineffable feeling of affection and solicitude toward a person, such as that arising from kinship, recognition of attractive qualities, or a sense of underlying oneness.

Again, those words can only be understood to the extent we can *feel* the feeling they describe. The same is true for other fundamental experiences, such as color; a definition of color can only have meaning for those who can see (or at least, have seen). For example, the same dictionary gives this definition for "red":

The hue of the long-wave end of the visible spectrum, evoked in the human observer by radiant energy with wavelengths of approximately 630 to 750 nanometers; any of a group of colors that may vary in lightness and saturation and whose hue resembles that of blood; one of the additive or light primaries; one of the psychological primary hues.

Here also the words mean little to those who have not had the experience.

Even *similar* experience is not enough to let us understand something we have no actual experience of (although in some cases it may come very close). People with red-green color-blindness know the color blue, for example, but does that mean they can understand the color green? Their brains are capable of the feat, but without their retinas ever providing the information to their brains, they will never experience what we call "green," and it seems unlikely that they will understand the color green in any substantial way. Certainly, such a person will know, intellectually, that "green is a color," but beyond that—what can the color-blind person know about "green" other than that, to him or her, it appears the same as "red?"

The experience of love, like the experience of a color or any other fundamental experience, simply cannot be defined to someone who does not already know it. This is why there can be so much confusion about something so basic in human life; the word "love" can be fully understood only by those who have in fact been loved, early enough and long enough to preserve at least some of their own emotional health.

Here, as with other states of being (and to quote psychologist Arthur Janov), *meaning is feeling.* A lack of feeling thus creates a meaningless life. In contrast, a healthy openness to natural feeling allows the meaning of life to be obvious; that meaning is an integral, unquestioned part of oneself. A healthy dog understands the meaning of life, as it understands love, and fear, and joy. It really should be no surprise (although it apparently is to many people) that a healthy person is at least as smart as a dog, in this area as in most others.

– 3 –

Improving Our Ability to Love

DESPITE THE DIFFICULTY of opening up to love after having been shut down to it, some people *can*, to some extent, improve their ability to feel love for others. Working with the amount of love we *do* experience, we can try to be more open to that feeling. We can actively seek to feel and to express more compassion for others, and to give in less often to whatever prevents us from doing so.

Working to improve our ability to love is precisely what Buddhism, Jainism, Christianity, and many other religions urge us to do, and for good reason. Within whatever defenses we have, there is a range of attitudes and levels of openness we can express and experience. Healthier actions and attitudes, within our personal limits, are better than less healthy ones. More love is better than less love.

Describing *why* this is so requires delving into our second definition of "love."

– 4 –

AN OBJECTIVE DEFINITION

An objective definition is one based on what we can see; on what happens. Such a definition for "love" might be:

Loving behavior is the behavior shown toward a person by someone who loves that person.

As true as that is, it is not detailed enough for our purposes. Suppose someone had never had a truly loving parent, or even seen one in action—what then?

– 5 –

IN THE NATURAL SCHEME of things, the feeling of love causes one to behave in a particular way towards the object of that love. This, one assumes, is why love evolved in the first place. Even carnivores display love (ask any dog- or cat-owner) and clearly regulate family and other social behavior in part by means of love and other feeling.

When the level of emotional health is high, the regulation of behavior by love and other feelings works quite well. When the level is low, it fails miserably.

Indeed, **feelings are the guideposts to appropriate behavior**—not only here, but generally. Appropriate regulation of social behavior is largely what our feelings are *for.*

When natural access to feeling is disrupted, behavior is also disrupted. For example, you would think balancing the parents' needs and the child's would be easy and natural. Certainly, parents in other species don't seem to have any problem with it—as long as their natural openness to feeling is not disrupted. Animals do have problems, however, if the parents had bad parenting *themselves,* or suffered some other early trauma. In that case, the animals often make terrible parents.[32]

If a dog or a cat can be an appropriate parent without reading half a dozen books by experts on the topic, a human being can, too. But here again, the key is emotional health: a parent who received plenty of love and affection early in life, and who is otherwise undamaged enough to have remained mostly open to feeling, will feel love for his or her child without the complicating and corrupting influence of repressed trauma and will behave accordingly. A parent who was less fortunate and who is, therefore, less open and more neurotic, will not behave as appropriately.

Interestingly, the experience of *showing loving behavior* towards others can perhaps *make us more loving*—that is, it can increase the chances of our showing loving behavior in the future and perhaps increase our ability to *feel* love as well. There are several possible reasons for this, including positive feedback involving response by the loved person, oxytocin production in the brain, and so on. (Oxytocin is a brain chemical associated with love and bonding.)

For example, after collecting data on 7,695 mothers over a period of fourteen years, Dr. Lane Strathearn found that moms who breast-fed longer were less likely to neglect or abuse their children later. Shorter time breast-feeding correlated with both increased frequency and greater severity of later abuse or neglect.

The mothers who breast-fed their babies, in short, displayed more loving behavior towards the children—during *and after* infancy. The effect was highly significant; in fact, the strongest predictor of future abuse in this large study was a breast-feeding time of less than four months.*

Dr. Strathearn points out that there are several factors at work here; for instance, a woman who was abused as a child is more likely to abuse her own children, and may also be less likely to breast-feed them. On the other hand, studies also show that a close, loving relationship at the earliest time of life (as comes in part from being breast-fed) can increase the number of oxytocin receptors in the brain, leading that person to benefit more from oxytocin production later in life—that is, to actually feel more love, more easily, than might someone who was less fortunate as an infant.[33]

---

* This does not imply that a mother who bottle-feeds her infant will later abuse that child, any more than the statistical fact of women being shorter than men says anything about the height of a particular man or woman. Statistical data about a large group (other than a datum which describes 100 percent of the group) says nothing about characteristics of an individual.

– 6 –

Interlude: Dogs

PEOPLE LOVE DOGS in part because dogs remind us of life's primal qualities, including the seeming contradictions built into life itself.

Dogs are loving, affectionate animals *and* cold-hearted killers. Their deep lungs, explosive running speed, powerful jaws, teeth designed to rip flesh, and digestive tracts designed mostly for raw meat remind us that dogs are hunters: they kill other animals to eat and survive. Of course, dogs are omnivores (unlike cats, which are almost pure carnivores), but the point remains that killing other animals is natural and commonplace for wild dogs and wolves. Ancestors of the dog who licks your hand and who clearly adores you, to the point of dying in your defense if necessary, may have hunted down, killed, and devoured ancestors of your own.

It is emotionally difficult to see these two opposing natures as part of a single whole. How can they coexist? Why would they evolve together? (Or, from another viewpoint: why would a Creator design animals with strong instincts both for love and for killing?)

Love coexists with the instincts for hunting, killing, and violently defending because each contributes to the survival of the species.

Without the tools and instincts to defend themselves and to hunt down and kill prey, wolves and other predators would not survive. It is easy to forget, especially if one lives in an urban environment, how pervasive hunting and killing are in the natural world. Likewise, starvation, disease, parasites, and simple thirst claim thousands of lives in the natural world every day. Every *minute*, actually.

Biologist Richard Dawkins points out that the amount of suffering in the natural world "is beyond all decent contemplation."[34] Certainly the phrase "predator and prey" defines much of the character of life in the natural world.

All the more amazing, then, that love even *became* a part of this world in the first place.

Yet we *do* have the capacity for love, and the *need* for love, because love is a critically important element in life. Seen most clearly and deeply in mammals, love seems an extension of the protective instinct and of various other social instincts found in lower lifeforms. Without such instincts, social life and procreation itself would be impossible. Mammals have expanded and developed these instincts to a depth that transforms the nature of experience. Just as the sense of hearing or of sight opens up a vast layer of experience, *love* brings entirely new areas of experience into being. Love changes the tone and texture of life and guides behavior in important ways.

As always, *words about an experience* are not the same as the experience itself. The more one opens up to the experience of love, the deeper one's understanding becomes.

I was reminded of this frequently after my wife and I adopted an adult Papillon whose former owner had died. It took time for us to warm up to the dog, to understand his rhythms and viewpoints, and to learn what he needed or expected from us. It took time for us to fully accept him and for him to accept us.

Within months, though, our relationship had been transformed, partly by simple knowledge of each other and most importantly by the beginnings of love. Six years later, as old age and multiple organ failure brought him to the end of his life, the depth of my feeling for this small animal was surprising, even to me. After he died, I wrote this to a friend:

> *He was upbeat and smiling all the way to the end; I stayed up with him all night and it was clear he felt happy to be with me, part of the pack, and that this was more important than the discomfort he was feeling. More than anything else, my time with Prince deepened my understanding of the importance of a loving attachment, and his passing has emphasized this even more.*
>
> *For instance, when I think of getting another dog, what immediately hits me is all the WORK this would involve: all the time caring for him in various ways, dealing with illnesses and other problems, dealing with the new dog's quirks and*

problem behaviors, grooming him, getting up in the middle of the night to take him out or whatnot (in the last six months with Prince, I was incredibly sleep-deprived), having to decide not to go to dinner or a movie in many cases, and so on.

It is a lot of work to have a dog. With Prince it never felt that way, because I loved him and that completely changed the texture of it all. Likewise, many of the original "problems" and irritations—dog hair everywhere, dog drool on my car windows, having to clean his paws after he'd been out in the dirt or gravel, concern over whether he'd mess up our carpet, and a hundred other things—all became invisible and much of it actually became heartwarming. I still feel a burst of affection when I find some of Prince's hair somewhere.

The saying is true: Love changes everything.

PRINCE THE WONDER DOG
October 1990 – April 2003

– 7 –

LOVE INCLUDES RESPECT FOR OTHERS

Perhaps as essential as the assumption of innate sociality in children and adults is a respect for each individual as his own proprietor.

The notion of ownership of other persons is absent among the Yequana. . . . Deciding what another person should do, no matter what his age, is outside the Yequana vocabulary of behaviors. There is great interest in what everyone does, but no impulse to influence—let alone coerce—anyone.

— *Jean Liedloff,* The Continuum Concept: In Search of Happiness Lost

THE TITLE OF LIEDLOFF'S BOOK refers to her idea that humans, like all species, necessarily have built-in expectations and needs—part of a continuum that informs and guides us and which we ignore to our detriment.

A human baby knows what to expect—not intellectually, but on a deeper level—because those expectations are carved into its own DNA. The baby expects to be cared for in a certain way, handled in a certain way, fed and kept warm and protected, and to otherwise have its needs tended to. A human baby can do none of that for itself; it can cry or wriggle to get attention, but the mother or *someone* must do the rest. That expectation is met, or the infant dies. Thus are the continuum and its expectations passed along through time.

A gray area exists where the child's needs are met only partially: well enough for life to continue; poorly enough that damage is done.

This is the default situation of mankind. *Changing that situation* is the most important task of the twenty-first century.

One of our needs is for the *freedom* to make our own choices and live our own lives. Freedom also enables harmony, in part because those whose freedom is respected in childhood find it easy to respect others in adulthood.

– 8 –

LOVE DOES NOT REQUIRE focusing on the other person (even an infant) to the near-exclusion of everything else. As Jean Liedloff (quoted above) points out,[35] it is natural and healthy for adults to care for their young without fawning over them to the point of

either neglecting adult needs and duties or confusing and trauma-
tizing the child with over-attention.

What Liedloff observed among the Yequana tribe of the
Amazon—and what she says works today, for her clients in the
United States—is parents going about their business with the child
nearby or carried in arms. The child is not the focus; the adult
attends to whatever she or he is normally doing. This lets the child
be a part of daily life, observing and learning and feeling that he or
she is a part of the family and the larger group—while *not* being
assaulted with more attention than is appropriate. Always nearby
yet not in the way, the child can communicate its needs, and have
those needs attended to by parents (and sometimes others) in a
natural and usually good-natured fashion.

– 9 –

WHEN CHILDREN are allowed authority over their own lives—as in
the Yequana tribe, and at Summerhill School and Sudbury Valley
School, of which more in Chapter 12—they grow up not only without fear of responsibility, but without either desire or willingness to
abandon their own responsibility (and thus authority over their
own lives) to someone else. Free and responsible children become
free and responsible adults.

To expect that unfree children will become free, responsible
adults is to expect the unlikely. *Some* people can overcome such
mistreatment from childhood, but we'd be fools to think very *many*
of them would do so.

Compassion for children requires giving them the same respect
and control over their own actions that we want ourselves, abro-
gating this only when consideration of the child's abilities and
needs truly require it.

– 10 –

WHILE THERE ARE MANY THINGS that can be done to improve the
lives of children, improvements in parenting are among the most

critical. Without some level of improvement here, the Paradise Paradigm will not succeed. If parents are entirely unwilling or unable to be *better* parents, there will be little or no improvement in the emotional health of their children, and the gradual increase in compassion and emotional health we are hoping for will not materialize. "Parenting" begins even before conception, of course; having children for the right reasons, not smoking or using other drugs during pregnancy, good prenatal care, planning for a safe and gentle birth experience, and many other things are important in determining the quality of life for the child.

The nature of neurosis works against positive change; the energy driving neurotic symptoms does not go away by itself. Feeling and connecting the traumatic events that underlie defenses are required for deep, genuine improvement, and very few parents will even consider doing such a thing. A defense system remains active until the feelings being defended against are fully felt and connected to consciousness. Since the defenses themselves work to prevent old feelings from being felt and connected, it becomes obvious why neurosis does not heal on its own or simply fade away.*

Neurosis and neurotic societies have been self-perpetuating for thousands of years for precisely that reason. Breaking this ancient cycle is the only hope for real improvement in the human condition—and perhaps the only hope for long-term continuation of the human race.

– *11* –

WHAT OF OUR OBJECTIVE DEFINITION? We might amend it to this:

Loving behavior exhibits sensitive consideration for the real needs and feelings of the loved person, in a way that benefits that person.

---

* Again, see Appendices 1, 3, and 4 for more detail on this topic.

In short, to love someone means to meet that person's real needs, in a way that is healthy for them—in every sense of the term. I mentioned in the previous chapter that children who suffer less abuse are *physically healthier later in life*, by a significant margin, than those who experience more abuse. The large ACE Study, for example, with over 17,000 participants (see article by Dr. Vincent Felitti in Appendix Four) found that four or more categories of abuse or distress in childhood more than *doubled* the likelihood of smoking in adulthood. Such children were (in their adulthood) also more than twice as likely to have chronic obstructive pulmonary disease, and twelve times times more likely to attempt suicide. (Participants with even higher ACE Scores were as much as *fifty-one times* more likely to attempt suicide). Dr. Felitti writes: "In addition to these examples, we found many other measures of adult health have a strong, graded relationship to what happened in childhood: heart disease, fractures, diabetes, obesity, unintended pregnancy, sexually transmitted diseases, and alcoholism were more frequent. Occupational health and job performance worsened progressively as the ACE Score increased." Subjects in the study were an average of fifty-seven years old, yet experiences from childhood were still having profound effects on their health and quality of life. This study is a powerful reminder that neurosis does not simply fade away or heal on its own.

The study above, along with many others, shows directly that love, given early in life, translates into a healthier later life. The level of protection conferred by early love is stunning; *any drug that had such a dramatic effect in lowering the risk of cancer, heart disease, and other problems would be hailed as a medical miracle.* This is in addition to the protection against criminal and other negative behavior.

Love is, indeed, a powerful force—when given early enough, and consistently.

Love is not merely a feeling (much less only a concept): it is a basic requirement for healthy human life.

– 12 –

Reasons for Optimism

As overwhelming as the task appears, there *are* reasons for optimism. For one thing, most parents want to do right by their children and are willing to sacrifice much to do so. For another, there are many *simple* things that can be done to improve the lives of children, including critically important things that, by themselves, can make a world of difference.

In particular, proper prenatal care,[36] a compassionate and gentle birth,[37] and breast-feeding for the first year or more—two years or longer, if possible[38]—provide a solid foundation for the child. Love throughout this period makes the child stronger yet softer; it provides a powerful foundation for handling later trauma and, by making the child more content and pleasant to be with, actually tends to *help* the parents be more loving.

In contrast, a child who is miserable inside may get less benefit from love he or she *does* get; when everything is experienced through a lens of misery and unhappiness, it is easy to miss positive events even when they are happening.

People with a *background emotional tone* of misery or fear or unhappiness tend to experience even *good* things as miserable or frightening or unpleasant.

In contrast, people whose needs have been met tend to experience things in a more accurate light, and to easily accept and experience love from others for what it is.

Adequate love early in life not only gives a person the tools to be a good parent later on: it also makes each and every day better than it otherwise would have been. A *lack* of early love ruins one's life; receiving love fulfills it.

SECTION THREE

THE ROAD TO PARADISE

CHAPTER 10

POSITIVE ACTION

*An invasion of armies can be resisted, but not an idea whose time
has come.*

— *Victor Hugo*

We have it in our power to begin the world over again.

— *Thomas Paine*

H OW DO WE GET THERE from here?
A healthy world—an Earthly Paradise—will be a world of
widespread emotional health, and of sufficient freedom from
government and other coercion to not merely allow but to *foster*
continued improvement in emotional health.

No single program or plan will get us there. Indeed, no program, no charitable foundation, no government agency, no group
or organization—*nothing*—will succeed at truly saving the world,
in the sense we have discussed, unless and until the *paradigm itself*
is very widely embraced.

It needn't be called "The Paradise Paradigm," but this same basic set of ideas, under whatever name, must become as commonly understood as, for example, the germ theory of disease. It must become embedded in the consciousness of people worldwide, and not only in the minds of academics or of some other specialized minority.

Why? The most important reason is *scale*: the task is simply too large to accomplish any other way. Paradigms do what lesser tools cannot: they harness the power of as many people as needed, over as long a time as necessary, to get the job done. Paradigms can act across decades and generations; across centuries. Some—those carried down through time by certain religions, for example—have been at work for literally thousands of years.

– 2 –

WHAT CAN YOU, personally, do to help move the world towards more health and compassion? For a start, promote the idea. Talk about it with friends. Add a link to *http://www.paradise-paradigm.net* at your website. Pass this book along to someone else after you read it. Let people know that a world with more love and compassion is possible, that people are thinking about such a world seriously, and that there is a way to move things in the right direction.

"Raising enough emotionally healthy children will create a healthy world." Say those words when you talk about the idea; it is important that people understand the basics. The point is to help people connect the dots: that

the nature of the human world
—is created largely by our—
treatment of the young.

There *is* a connection, and it is neither vague nor uncertain. One must also be clear, when talking about the Paradigm, that *imposing it by force* (including by government programs) is literally *counterproductive* instead of merely inefficient.

That is so because, to say it again, *love and freedom require each other.* I have discussed that truth in some detail already, but it is the point that people most often have trouble understanding. Point 6 of the Paradigm is worth repeating here:

> *Freedom is a necessary part of love. Unfreedom (coercion) is abuse; it erodes and destroys love.*

Examples are everywhere; you need only look to see them. Even the best ideas for improving the world only cause harm in the long run when implemented with coercion.

– 3 –

OF COURSE, you may want to do more. Many will have specific ideas about how to increase love and compassion. Again, it is this factor—millions of people working on the problem, instead of one bureaucrat or agency designing a program from afar—that gives paradigms their astonishing power. Paradigms do what top-down, authoritarian, centralized systems cannot—can *never*—do.

Below is a list of ideas to get you started on your own list. The point of each item is to improve the world, and especially the quality of life for one or more people, in some way. This list, I hope, will stimulate your own thoughts on what could be done.

You will have different ideas, including, surely, some that would never occur to me. You will have different strengths and talents than I do, and different viewpoints, different circles of influence, different interests.

Imagine how total our failure would be otherwise. I earnestly hope this book will be a factor in moving millions of people to actions, large and small, that will begin the process of healing the world. But if everyone did what I did, we'd have millions of books like this one, by millions of authors, and not enough of anything else.

We need more than that. Fortunately, we have the talents and energy of not millions of people to draw upon, but of billions.

As we saw in Chapter 2, society itself is an emergent system.

Spreading control and action across the entire organism (cells in a body; bees in a hive; people in a society) provides the best use of resources, including of information, which is often local in nature and rapidly changing. The underlying power of distributed, emergent systems is woven into the fabric of the universe; paradigms are simply a way to harness and partially direct that power in human society.

"Change happens when enough people share the necessary understanding."

– 4 –

Quick Review

First, let us review what we are trying to do. Working backward:

THE LONG-TERM GOAL IS A MORE HEALTHY, FREE, AND LOVING WORLD.

We want enough change to end war, to put a permanent stop to government atrocity against innocents, to rid the world of racism, violent crime, drug addiction, and all the other symptoms, large and small, that currently stem from widespread early trauma—from neurosis. We've gotten over our shock at such a large idea and are considering ways to move the world in the right direction.

– 5 –

TO ATTAIN THAT GOAL, WE NEED A LARGE MAJORITY OF FREE AND EMOTIONALLY HEALTHY ADULTS.

Ultimately, we want *all* adults in the world to be free and emotionally healthy. That may be unrealistic and unattainable, but if so, then we want the largest possible percentage of adults to be free and emotionally healthy.

While "the more the better," of course, we do not know what percentage will be required for major, long-term change. What percentage of repressed and angry adults can turn a civilized nation into a Nazi Germany, a Red China, a North Korea, a Cambodia under the Khmer Rouge? Clearly, some percentage of people in a nation can be healthy and non-violent even as the cancer of totalitarianism grows. The trains may run on time; the economy may be in fine shape; the average person may not yet feel the rough hand of the police state, but that may only make it harder for people to see what is happening. Not everyone need be a monster for monsters to reign.

So again: a large, if unknown, percentage of the population must be both free and emotionally healthy, if the world is to be saved. If enough people understand that idea, and given enough time, we can make a difference—enough to change the world for the better. My hope and belief is that we can permanently transform the world, in the most positive way imaginable, and to an extent we scarcely dare dream of today. I hope that by now you share this belief.

– 6 –

SUCH A WORLD—where freedom and healthy, loving adults are the norm—REQUIRES FIRST THAT PREGNANT MOTHERS, INFANTS, AND CHILDREN BE TREATED WITH LOVE, COMPASSION, AND RESPECT.

Their needs, both physical and emotional, must be met widely and consistently. A child raised with love and compassion, and whose physical and emotional needs are met from the start (from conception), becomes a loving, compassionate adult—one who finds it easy and natural to meet the physical and emotional needs of *his or her* children.

A child treated with respect—allowed to exercise sovereignty in her own actions, allowed to think and feel for himself, while being taught (without cruelty) to give equal respect to others—becomes a responsible and respectable adult who respects others.

In this way, and for this reason, such a world will be self-sustaining, just as the neurotic world has been self-sustaining for millennia.

– 7 –

IMPROVING THE LIVES OF PREGNANT MOTHERS, INFANTS, AND CHILDREN REQUIRES THAT TODAY'S (and tomorrow's) ADULTS DO, ON AVERAGE, A BETTER JOB WITH THEIR CHILDREN THAN THEIR PARENTS DID WITH THEM.

The quicker this happens, the better, but we must not let ourselves be discouraged by the long-term character of the project. Because the nature of complex systems is for very early experience to have great impact, small, positive changes at the start of life can translate into large improvements in that infant's lifelong emotional health. A gentle birth, for example (see—please—<u>Birth Without Violence</u> by Dr. Frederick Leboyer) can improve someone's entire life, giving them strength to meet later traumas and providing a deep feeling of compassion and connection with others. The point is that parents need not become super-human or more healthy than they already are to improve the lives of their children. A few simple actions can make a world of difference.

– 8 –

IN ORDER FOR TODAY'S (and tomorrow's) ADULTS TO IMPROVE THEIR TREATMENT OF PREGNANT MOTHERS, INFANTS, AND CHILDREN, THEY MUST WIDELY HEAR THE MESSAGE, AND LEARN THE LESSON, THAT *RAISING ENOUGH EMOTIONALLY HEALTHY CHILDREN WILL CREATE A HEALTHY WORLD.*

They must also hear and learn some of the detail of this truth, but most important is that they begin to see and to feel the connection between treatment of the young, and the state of the world itself.

People must know not only that individual adults live better, healthier, and more compassionate lives when they have been raised with love and compassion and freedom, but that entire families, and villages, and societies, and states and nations, and the world itself will be improved by that method. Groups (including the world as a whole) have, and can only have, the composite character of the people who make up those groups.

In short, people must know that our treatment of children, of infants, and of pregnant women determines the actual character of the world: concentration camp or Paradise; blood-soaked killing field or compassionate brotherhood; corrupt police-state or free and honest marketplace; polluted and dying environment or an Earth cared for by people in touch with their feelings—including their feelings for nature, for each other, and for everything that lives.

– 9 –

Suggestions for positive action:

○ **Resolve to treat your own children with all the love, compassion, and respect that you wish you, yourself, had been treated with as a child** (whether you were so treated or not). This does not mean letting children harm others; it does not rule out being firm (but never cruel or mean spirited) when appropriate. It does mean allowing for the nature of children, and for the unique character of each specific child. Children are noisy, and messy, and often more energetic than adults wish they were. That is in the nature of being a child. Consider that to disapprove of someone's basic nature is to disapprove of him or her personally. Books and other resources that may be helpful are in the *Further Reading* section.

○ **Do the simple, compassionate, and critically important things right at the start:**
  • **Get proper nutrition** if you are, or if there is even a chance that you will become, pregnant.
  • **See your doctor for prenatal care, if possible.**
  • Follow your doctor's advice to **not smoke, drink, or use other unnecessary drugs** during your pregnancy.

- **Plan for a gentle birth.** If a C-section or other medical intervention is necessary, give the new baby as much affectionate contact as possible, as soon as possible.
- **Breast-feed your baby.** Continue for two to three years or more, if at all possible. The advantages are many. In addition to enhancing bonding and attachment (critical for lifelong emotional health), physical health benefits for both the child and the mother are well documented.
- **Do not banish your child to solitary confinement;** sleep in the same bed or at least in the same room as your infant or young child whenever possible. Nearly all mammals sleep together with their young, and it has been the norm throughout most of human history. Westerners will often let the family dog sleep in bed with them, but not their own children. That is more than passing strange, is it not? While *some* adults should never be in the same bed (or room, for that matter) with children, that does not mean parents in general should be (literally) distant from their own offspring at night.
- **Remember that love includes freedom.** Authoritarianism is tyranny; it is a form of unlove, in a family as in a nation. A natural sense of responsibility comes from the freedom to live our own lives, to make our own decisions, and to experience the consequences (good and bad) accordingly. Far less parental direction is needed than most people imagine or believe. The "Further Reading" section of this book includes several titles that document this truth in detail, and which provide vivid accounts of how well freedom for children works.
- **Remember also that license is not freedom;** that is, the right to make one's own decisions does not include the right to infringe on the equal rights of others. Neither an adult nor a child has any right to initiate coercion against another, for example—either directly or by proxy.

○ **Stay as open to your own true feelings as you can.**

○ **The difficult part of staying open is to not put old feelings** (i.e., feelings that were never allowed to become fully conscious) **onto people in the present.** For example, if you carry (repressed, childhood) anger towards one of your parents, try not to direct *that* anger toward your children, spouse, or others in the present. It may not be possible to do this perfectly, or consistently, but to the extent that you *can* manage this feat, you will be doing something positive. If you can feel the original feeling (whatever it is) fully, whether in therapy or not, then all the better, but the point is to be open to feeling without inflicting *old* feelings upon those in the present—especially upon children.

○ **Insure that communication stays open** as your children grow—between parents and children, and between the parents themselves.

○ **Revisit the premise of the Paradise Paradigm,** by re-reading some or all of the book occasionally, by visiting the website (*http://www.paradise-paradigm.net/*), by discussing it with someone (your children perhaps) or by simply reviewing it in your mind.

○ **Spread the concept.** Progress towards the goal requires harnessing the power unique to paradigms. Many people— very many, at some point—must understand at least enough of the basic idea for their behavior to change, however slightly, toward what is needed.

○ **Read other books and articles that relate to the goal.** "Saving the world" is a big topic; the solution will necessarily involve many sub-topics. The "Further Reading" section in the back of this book is a good place to start, but you will find (and already know of, for that matter) many other sources worth reading.

○ **Support groups that work to improve the lives of pregnant mothers, babies, infants, or children.** There are thousands of such groups; find one that appeals to you and that is well-run, and support it in whatever way you want and can.

○ **Break the cycle.** If you feel you need help with your behavior, seek assistance.

○ **Support human rights and restricted government power in general.** No other tool than government allows for, not to mention *encourages*, mass murder and torture on the scale that so many governments have been guilty of throughout history. Any system based entirely on force, and which enables as much murder and mayhem as government, is *not* a positive force for love and compassion.

○ **Create a legacy.** Part of the meaning of each person's life lies in the effects that person has on future generations. This is clear enough for parents, but everyone, parent or not, has an effect on the world and on those who come after. *The Paradise Paradigm* is an invitation to consider your own life in this context, and to be, in your own way, a force for positive change.

— *10* —

"Raising enough emotionally-healthy children will create a healthy world."

Pass it on.

CHAPTER 11

OBSTACLES AND DANGERS:
OPPOSITION TO LOVE
AND FREEDOM

As soon as there is life there is danger.

— *Ralph Waldo Emerson*

PARADISE HAS NOT YET been widely and permanently created on Earth for a good reason: the time has not been right.

Conditions allowing for widespread, on-going emotional health have simply not been available to most human beings since we came down out of the trees. The average life expectancy for our species during prehistoric times may have been as little as nineteen years. So many people died in childbirth (mothers and newborns alike), during infancy, in childhood, and in their teens that despite some people living to be grandparents, the average lifespan—whatever the actual number—was shockingly, horrifyingly low during most of our time on this planet. The amount of grief, fear, and pain caused by problems at birth, infectious disease, predators, human conflict, hunger, and poor conditions of sanitation and housing, among other things, made repression of trauma an on-going necessity.

"Repression of trauma" is the start of neurosis and the end of deep, natural connection to feeling. For an individual, *neurosis is the end of Paradise.* Widespread neurosis is the end of Paradise for a society or a world.

– 2 –

PREDICTING THE FUTURE is always a gamble; we cannot reliably predict the flip of a coin, much less the future of complex, global systems.

Still, it is in our nature to try.

Prediction is even more difficult than in the past because we are at the edge of a massive discontinuity—an unprecedented break in human history, with many quite different possible futures streaming out ahead of us. The ever-growing tidal wave of human knowledge is creating new possibilities, new realities, new futures, roiling beneath the surface of the present.

The divergent nature of these many possible futures means that the character of the future we actually encounter is more uncertain than at perhaps any time in human history. Even if we seem clearly headed down one path, a new discovery or invention or social event could quickly bump us into a very different path.

Whatever our path turns out to be, it almost surely will be a bumpy one.

– 3 –

HERE IS AN OPTIMISTIC THOUGHT for this somewhat pessimistic chapter: a healthier world might actually be inevitable. The amazing improvement in health, average lifespan, and material wealth over history, which has accelerated greatly in recent decades, certainly suggests that possibility.

Modern technology and other factors have already had a powerful, positive impact, and this trend might insure that, despite the commonplace horrors of today, a healthier world will eventually emerge, regardless of any plan, paradigm, or other specific effort, and despite the crime, tyranny, and other misery we read about in our daily newspapers.

Certainly, our technology has advanced in ways that *have* benefited us for the most part. Ray Kurzweil, famous for creating the Kurzweil Reading Machine and other technology, believes the beneficial character of technology's advance is likely to continue—and, for that matter, to rapidly exceed anything most people can even imagine. Kurzweil holds awards from Carnegie Mellon and MIT, and his writings on the future, including 1990's The Age of Intelligent Machines, are popular and widely respected.

Kurzweil is clearly enamored of the future; he conveys a powerfully upbeat feeling about where things are headed. Elimination of that pesky "death" problem is only one of the reasons you'll be happy to live in the future he sees—assuming things go as planned.

– 4 –

OF COURSE, things may go differently—from this early vantage point, we cannot know. In any case, there *are* trends opposing such rosy predictions, and they are the focus of this chapter.

Indeed, many obstacles and counter-forces are at work. These may not only have prevented Paradise from emerging yet: they may be strong enough to permanently block it, or even to move the world in the opposite direction.

As melodramatic as that sounds, it is not impossible.

Bill Joy is among those worried about the more extreme dangers of technology, and he (like Kurzweil) understands the problem better than most. Joy coauthored the Java Language Specification and cofounded Sun Microsystems. This man's opinions on the benefits and dangers of modern technology are at least worth considering—and, in stark contrast to Kurzweil, he is frightened.

In "Why the Future Doesn't Need Us" (*Wired Magazine*, April 2000[39]) Joy describes his concerns for the near future. They include especially "knowledge-based mass destruction"—"KMD"—and in particular, genetics, nano-tech, and robotics: technologies that will soon be within the grasp of individuals and small groups.

Building a nuclear bomb from scratch requires a huge effort, expensive equipment, many skilled and unskilled workers, and millions or even billions of dollars. But a genetically engineered super-virus or a self-replicating nano-plague could be made, it appears, with little money or equipment. A wealthy individual, and eventually even a disaffected middle-class teenager, could produce such a weapon.

Such possibility is no longer distant. The exponential growth of human knowledge means that the next century will bring more change than Mankind has seen before in all of history combined. Like it or not, a new world *is* coming.

When the emotionally damaged kid down the street can build, not a computer virus, but a *real* virus designed to kill millions—then we had better not have too many emotionally damaged children. When an unhappy, precocious teenager (not to mention even the smallest of governments) can loose a nano-plague of malicious self-replicating micro-bots into the world, then the world had better be a far more healthy place than it is now.

Bill Joy is not the only person concerned about the combination of twenty-first century technology and continued, widespread emotional damage. Princeton astrophysicist (and England's Royal Astronomer) Martin Rees has a standing bet (stake: $1,000) that "Bioterror, or bioerror, will lead to one million casualties in a single event by 2020."[40] He is specifically concerned about "individual weirdos" as well as organizations of various sizes. So far, no one has been willing to bet against him. And Rees' 2003 book <u>Our Final Hour</u> is cheerfully subtitled <u>A scientist's warning: How terror, error, and environmental disaster threaten humankind's future in this century—on Earth and beyond</u>.

Such commentary raises two important points for us: first, it emphasizes (by implication if not directly) the importance of increasing the levels of emotional health in the world; mankind literally may not survive the combination of widespread neurosis, coercive government power, and twenty-first century technology.

Science lets people do things that were not possible previously, but our emotional health determines *what* we decide to do with the new, ever-increasing power that science creates. A psychopath with a spear or a rifle is one thing; a psychopath who can design and build an invisible, contagious, and deadly super-virus is quite another.

The second point suggested by Joy's and Rees' concerns for the near future is that the balance between good and evil may not be what we think, and in any case is shifting in ways we cannot predict. Assuming that the world is moving in the right direction—that human progress is inevitable—could be a mistake. We do not, and cannot, know for certain how things will turn out.

– 5 –

WHAT FORCES—other than technology run amok combined with emotional damage and, in the worst cases, with centralized, coercive state power—might oppose the creation of a healthier world?

Plenty of them, unfortunately. Crime, greed, lust for power, and a hundred more. We considered several in earlier chapters.

Ultimately, most such factors come down to two issues: emotional health and our attitude towards "official" uses of coercion. We naturally think in terms of the *groups* and *actions* that we see, rather than in terms of the inner forces and fundamentals driving behavior and shaping organizations. But name any person, group, or trend that opposes compassion and freedom, and you will find, after careful thought, that *emotional damage* is indeed the problem—or at least a key part of it. Historically and into the present day, a substantial amount of that emotional damage is created, directly and indirectly, by government coercion, as we saw in Chapter 6. This is in addition to direct physical harm and danger created by coercive government, up to and including the danger of extinction events for the human species. For example, both nuclear and biological weapons—government programs, of course—have the potential to nearly or perhaps entirely wipe out the human race.

There *are* additional factors involved beyond the two (emotional health and coercive government power) we have focused on. For people genetically predisposed to violence or ruthlessness, for example—and it appears that some of us are—a good childhood is even *more* important, just as proper diet and exercise are even more important for someone predisposed to heart disease.

Genetic predisposition does not usually equal "fate" but it does mean that a condition is statistically more likely. Just how much more likely varies from "hardly at all" to "almost certain." I have seen nothing to suggest that serious criminality—rape or murder, for instance—is ever entirely the result of genetic factors.

Other factors working against love and freedom may be completely unexpected, even now. For example, in The Alphabet Versus the Goddess: The Conflict Between Word and Image (1998), Leonard Shlain suggests that *literacy,* including especially the widespread, frequent reading of alphabetic languages, may over-emphasize the major hemisphere of the brain, shifting thought, behavior, and social order in surprising ways. Among other things, this may, unless opposed by other factors, dramatically diminish the rights and standing of women in a society.

If something as commonplace as *literacy* might affect how people treat each other, who knows what other factors could be at work? And who knows what benefits we might see if enough people understood those factors?

Yet despite genetics, hemispheric-dominance imbalance, and anything else we might find, the evidence is clear and indisputable that *how infants and children (and even fetuses) are treated affects how they behave and experience life as adults.* Someone may be genetically prone to anti-social behavior, violence, or anything else, but what actualizes—in their later behavior and inner experience—will be shaped and colored by their early experience. Despite genetics and other factors, it is *love, compassion, and freedom* which bring out the best in us—and the *lack* of love, compassion and freedom which bring out the worst.

– 6 –

THE TWENTIETH CENTURY saw technology used repeatedly in the furtherance of evil—in wars, in nuclear arsenals, in the repression of entire societies, and inadvertently in the mechanization of birth, and of infant and child care. If Joy and Rees are correct about technology giving an even stronger hand to evil in the 21st century—and it is hard to see why that wouldn't be true—then working to improve the lives of infants, children, and pregnant mothers is more important than ever.

Machines may soon become intelligent *, and even surpass human intelligence, as Kurzweil and others believe. But those machines will not have human feelings—feelings built upon deep physiological, biological mechanisms that have evolved over millions of years for specific biological reasons.

As pointed out in Chapter 9, *feelings are the guideposts to appropriate behavior.* Without healthy access to our human feelings, we can behave as monsters—see any newspaper, any history book for how unfeeling humans (e.g., neurotics and especially sociopaths) can and do behave, thanks to repressed feeling.

How will unfeeling machines behave? Without emotionally healthy men and women programming them, I fear that Joy's vision may become reality. Even in the best case, the machines will soon enough be programming themselves, and eventually will bypass or grow beyond whatever restraints have been programmed into earlier generations. (And this is without even considering "grey goo" and other self-replicating nano-nightmares that Joy discusses.)

---

* Or not; researchers recently calculated the memory capacity of the human brain, focusing more on the number of connections than on the number of neurons, and by this measure your brain can hold more data than all the computers ever manufactured. "Brain beats all computers" by Roger Dobson, The London Independent, September 14, 2003

The good news is that sentient machines will not likely have old, repressed feelings that they are dealing with unconsciously in the present. The bad news is, they also won't have any human feeling or sensibility at all, beyond simulations that have been programmed into them and which may or may not be accurate or appropriate. Will they care about the same things we do? Will they have any reason to live in harmony with us? Time will tell. In the meantime, moving humanity in the direction of health, freedom, and love is the least we can do, and may be literally necessary to our species' survival.

CHAPTER 12

THE BENEFITS OF COMPASSION AND FREEDOM

I have seen children born to mothers who are very careful and loving in prebirth, birth, and afterward. These children are different. They are alert, smart, physically advanced, not sick, not whiny, creative, warm, and cuddly. Who would want more than that?
— *Arthur Janov* [41]

All truth passes through three stages. First, it is ridiculed. Second, it is violently opposed. Third, it is accepted as being self-evident.
— *Arthur Schopenhauer*

I HAVE FRIENDS FROM INDIA who are of the Jain religion. More than even Buddhism or Hinduism, Jainism focuses on the concept of *Ahimsa*: compassion and non-violence towards every living thing.

The practical results are interesting. Over the years, I have attended perhaps two dozen Jain gatherings, including parties, religious events, and other large get-togethers. Occasionally, a hundred people or more have been involved. Children and infants are always present at these gatherings.

I cannot recall any child crying or being "fussy" at one of these events. Nor do I remember ever hearing a Jain adult speak harshly to a child—or to anyone else, for that matter. And spanking or otherwise *hitting* a child, for any reason, would be unthinkable.

For that very reason—because the children are treated gently and with love from the start; because they are included in their parents' lives as much as possible; because they are seldom or never left in the care of strangers—these Jain children are a delight to be around. Their behavior does not grate on the nerves; quite the opposite.

This result is not a fluke. Dr. Frederick Leboyer, who wrote Birth Without Violence, spent time in India observing and learning from the birth practices there, and from the traditional ways that parents treat their infant children. These experiences led him to write two other books: Loving Hands: The Traditional Indian Art of Baby Massage and Inner Beauty, Inner Light: Yoga for Pregnant Women. Both contain many photographs of Indian mothers and children, which not only show how to perform the exercises Leboyer describes, but which convey a sense of gentleness, strength, calmness, and inner beauty.

– 2 –

A WORLD WHERE widespread neurosis and tyranny have given way to health and freedom will not come into being overnight. That is a difficult truth to accept, and it may help to know that a great deal of benefit will be seen along the way.

– 3 –

LOVING TREATMENT of infants and children has an immediate side-benefit: the babies and children are happier, and in turn easier to live with. This is in addition to the pleasure and contentment that comes from bonding and being close, emotionally as well as physically, to one's child (or to any other being, really, including the family dog).

The *attachment parenting* movement is one attempt to address this issue. Attachment parenting is a loose system involving just what it sounds like: being close to one's infant and child, physically and emotionally.

Among the more respected and prolific authors on the subject are Dr. William Sears and Mrs. Martha Sears, RN. Together, they host a website on attachment parenting and related issues (*http://www.askdrsears.com*) and have published more than two dozen books.

The Sears' description of attachment parenting includes this list, which they call the "Baby B's":

Birth bonding
Breast-feeding
Babywearing
Bedding close to baby
Belief in the language value of your baby's cry
Beware of baby trainers
Balance

What are the *results* of attachment parenting? Dr. and Mrs. Sears have found that children raised in this fashion are much as described by Dr. Janov in the quotation at the start of this chapter. Specifically, the Sears have found that "AP kids" tend to be:

Caring
Compassionate
Connected
Careful
Confident

In addition, the Sears find that *parents* of these children are more confident in their abilities as parents. They have been *connected* with their children from the start; learning from them instead of imposing an artificial agenda upon them.

It is an important point that the experience is improved for *both* parent and child.

It should be mentioned that something called "attachment

therapy" may involve coercion and severe physical restraint, and has apparently been implicated in the death of at least one child.* "Attachment parenting" as described and advocated by the Sears is nothing like the descriptions I have seen of "attachment therapy" despite the similar names.

– 4 –

COMPELLING EXAMPLES of how love and freedom inspire positive results in the here-and-now may also be found in the results of the free school movement. Schools that emphasize freedom for children include the famous Summerhill School in England and the American Sudbury Valley School, and other schools run on the Sudbury model. The dramatic levels of freedom and responsibility given to children at Summerhill and at Sudbury stand in amazing contrast to the coercion and dreary Big-Brotherism typical of modern government schooling. The results are equally impressive, especially in terms of character and quality of life.

This *level* of change is needed, and widely, if we are to eventually put an end to neurosis and its resulting horrors. Timid steps may serve as a start, but bold action *will* be required for real, long-lasting change.

For those not familiar with Summerhill School, I have reproduced the entire *British Government Inspectors' Report from 1949*, at the companion website for this book. The page is *http://www. paradise-paradigm.net/summerhill.htm*. A. S. Neill, who founded Summerhill School in 1921 and whose 1960 book <u>Summerhill: A Radical Approach To Child Rearing</u> was an international bestseller, included this report in his book about the school, and it serves well as a snapshot of the school and its staff and children, as seen by outsiders.

The book itself makes Neill's deep love and respect for children

---

* "Death by Theory: Attachment therapy is based on a pseudoscientific theory that, when put into practice, can be deadly", by Michael Shermer, *Scientific American*, June 2004

very apparent, and makes clear, for those ready to see on this topic, the connections among love, freedom, responsibility, and happiness.

Five points, taken verbatim from the text of the Inspectors' Report, are worth noting here. Again, these are the words of government inspectors, not Neill himself. (Emphasis added in the paragraphs below):

1. **"The main principle upon which the School is run is freedom.** . . . . the degree of freedom allowed to the children is very much greater than the inspectors had seen in any other school and the freedom is real. No child, for instance, is obliged to attend any lessons. As will be revealed later, the majority do attend for the most part regularly, but one pupil was actually at this School for 13 years without once attending a lesson and is now an expert toolmaker and precision instrument maker. This extreme case is mentioned to show that the freedom given to children is genuine and is not withdrawn as soon as its results become awkward."

2. **" . . . the children are full of life and zest.** Of boredom and apathy there was no sign. An atmosphere of contentment and tolerance pervades the School."

3. **" . . . the children's manners are delightful.** They may lack, here and there, some of the conventions of manners, but their friendliness, ease and naturalness, and their total lack of shyness and self-consciousness made them very easy, pleasant people to get on with."

4. **" . . . initiative, responsibility and integrity are all encouraged by the system** and that so far as such things can be judged, they are in fact being developed."

5. **"Summerhill education is not necessarily hostile to worldly success."**

The report backs up that last point with a list of degrees held and careers followed by former pupils. Clearly, the lack of a "normal," coercive education has not harmed the children of Summerhill.

More importantly, compared with typical schooling, Summerhill clearly produces—and has, for over 75 years—exactly the kind of people we would all want as neighbors.

– 5 –

AS MENTIONED, Sudbury Valley School in America, and other schools run on the same model, produce similar results to those described in the British Inspectors' Report on Summerhill.

Founded in 1968 in Massachusetts, Sudbury Valley School offers no formal classes other than those which students initiate by contracting with a staff member or other student. Fishing—all day, every day, for as many years as you care to do it—is a perfectly acceptable (and not unheard of) way for a student to spend his time.

Do the kids learn? Of course they do. Because they aren't being coerced to learn things they aren't interested in at the moment—because they aren't even coerced to learn what they *are* interested in—they learn quickly, easily, and thoroughly, when they feel ready to. How long does it take young kids to learn math, when they aren't being forced? About twenty contact hours, at an hour a week. That includes long division, fractions, decimals, percentages, and square roots, not just addition and subtraction. When founder Daniel Greenberg first put together a math class—for students who had asked for one, of course—he was amazed at how quickly the students learned. Decades later, he knows this was no fluke. Children who aren't coerced also learn to read with no problem, and often without any adult assistance. Nor do they develop dyslexia, which Greenberg says may afflict as many as twenty percent of children in public schools. The rate of dyslexia at Sudbury has been "zero."

When the time comes for college or a career, Sudbury students are not merely ready: after years of having been literally responsible for their own learning (and for their own actions generally), they are confident and competent. They know what they want and how to achieve it. Years of getting along with others in a setting where every person is free and responsible make them easy to be around.

Greenberg's <u>Free at Last: The Sudbury Valley School</u> is a good overview of the school and of what the school experience is like. It was written many years after the school opened, and a second edition was published in 1995. This isn't mere cranksterism or theory: it is the story of a working, non-government school which has spawned several other successful schools run on the same model.

<u>Free at Last</u> is well and simply written, yet nearly every page explodes a myth or teaches a startling lesson about what childhood could be, can be, and *must* be. If children are to grow up outside the mental and emotional prisons we now herd them into, schools like Sudbury Valley must become the norm instead of almost unknown curiosities.

If you have children, or are a child; if you care about children or about education generally; if you are curious about how astonishingly different life can be from what we have made of it, <u>Free at Last</u> and other books available about Sudbury School (or about Summerhill School) will be an invigorating visit to a world that feels so right, so real, so healthy and sane that you may not want to leave.

– 6 –

THERE ARE MANY other positive authors, groups, movements, and ideas in the area of healthier, non-coercive learning. Two examples are the "unschooling" movement and the writings of John Holt.

– 7 –

FOR A REMINDER OF WHAT public schools are often like, consider books and other writings by John Taylor Gatto (who taught for 30 years, was named New York State's "Teacher of the Year" in 1991 and was three times New York City's "Teacher of the Year") including <u>Dumbing Us Down: The Hidden Curriculum of Compulsory Schooling</u>.

In the United States, more than twenty percent of public school teachers now send their own children to private schools. This is about twice the rate at which parents in general send children to private schools, and in some parts of the country the figure is even higher. The *Washington Times* reported in 2004 that over twenty-five percent of Washington, D.C. public school teachers send their children to private schools. In Baltimore, the figure is thirty-five percent.[42]

When those who know government schools best, from the inside, are paying to get their own children out of that system—at twice the rate other parents do—it becomes clear that something is very wrong with coercive government education.

– 8 –

ONE MORE EDUCATIONAL OPTION deserves mention here: home schooling. In the United States, home schooling has grown from a small curiosity to a sizeable trend. In 1985, 50,000 American children were homeschooled; in 1996, the number was 1.2 million, according to the *Homeschool Legal Defense Association*. As this is written, the number may be closer to 2 million, or about 3.5 percent of all school-age children. The number of homeschooled American children today exceeds the total number of public school students in 41 of the 50 states combined.

Home schooling is by far the least expensive means of educating children—an important consideration in a nation which is technically bankrupt, as the United States is in the early years of the twenty-first century. At about $250 to $650 per child annually, home schooling costs less than a *tenth* of what a public school education costs—yet home schooling is far superior, both academically and in terms of the social skills imparted.[43] Home schooling is not for everyone, but with roughly 50 million students at America's public and private schools, the potential dollar savings is staggering, and the other benefits may be even more important.

– 9 –

AS CHILDREN TREATED with respect and compassion grow, they will continue, in general, to be healthier, more pleasant to live with, more caring of others, more confident in themselves, and less distracted by inner demons.

We know what they will be like, as a group, because hundreds of studies and thousands of case histories and other observations tell us that children who are loved and respected, who are allowed freedom in their lives, and who are otherwise not traumatized or abused, grow up just as you would expect them to: as compassionate, healthy, confident children who become compassionate, healthy, confident adults.

For example, *they will show lower rates of violence than the current norm.*

They will suffer lower rates of depression, suicide, and other forms and symptoms of inner misery.

They will be less likely to use drugs, to drink, or to smoke.

Partly for that reason (and partly for reasons of lower stress, regardless of drug use) *they will have lower rates of "neurotic-fueled" diseases, including cancer and heart disease.*

Having been free, responsible, and respected in childhood, *they will be free, responsible, and respectful of others as adults.*

Having not been abused themselves, *they will be far less likely to commit child abuse of any kind against their own children.*

Perhaps most importantly, by **being** healthier and raising healthier children, *they will move the world closer to a permanent shift in character: towards more compassion, more love, more freedom, more humanity—**towards Paradise.***

– 10 –

CHANGE GLINTS ON THE HORIZON, out of focus yet tantalizingly close. The old world is crumbling, and will be gone forever before we know it: technology and other factors ensure this. As a result, Paradise is coming, here in *this* world, or else the other extreme: hell on Earth.

Either is possible. The middle ground, where we expect to find ourselves, does not seem likely, at least to me. Nor is it worth aiming for.

Choosing *Paradise* requires us to bring more love, compassion, and freedom into the world, and especially into the world of the very young. It requires us to honor the true needs and desires of every child who emerges on this Earth—the same needs and desires that we have all been born with since the dawn of our kind.

At long last, the time has come to bring this new world into existence. We have the tools, including the most important one: a simple and usefully accurate paradigm. And we know *from experience* that paradigms work—that they actually do change the world.

Yet the window of opportunity for *ending neurosis and tyranny as the default condition of mankind* may be rapidly closing. Paradise will not rise from the ashes of a global thermonuclear war; it will not take root in a police state ruled by fear and coercion; it may not survive an extended, artificially enhanced superplague. The necessary conditions may not last as long as we think, or believe, or hope.

The stakes are epic: the character of the human world, and thus the quality of life for many billions of people over the coming years, and decades, and millennia.

– 11 –

WHAT COMES NEXT is up to you, and to all of us. Time is short, and the choices we face are simple:

Health or sickness.
Love or hate.
Compassion or cruelty.
Freedom or tyranny.
Now or never.

Appendix One

FURTHER READING

WHAT FOLLOWS is a short list of books on relevant topics, written, for the most part, with a popular audience in mind. My intent is to give you a place to find more information on topics discussed in this book, rather than to catalog every publication used in the preparation of this one. Comments, if any for a given selection, begin in **bold** type.

The exceptions to the "general audience" rule are Kuhn's dry and technical <u>Structure of Scientific Revolutions</u>, included because *Chapter 2* in *this* book made it unthinkable to leave Kuhn's classic off this list, and Stephen Wolfram's well-known and authoritative writings on complex systems, cellular automata, and related topics.

Several websites are also included. The content of websites often changes or even disappears, so what you find at these sites may not be what I encountered; such is the nature of the internet.

FEELINGS AND EMOTIONAL HEALTH:

<u>Birth Without Violence</u> by Frederick Leboyer, 1974, *Inner Traditions International Limited*; 2nd Revision edition 2002. **What is the**

meaning of "sensitive dependence on early conditions" in human life? <u>Birth Without Violence</u> is among the best starting points for answering that question.

<u>The Continuum Concept: In Search of Happiness Lost</u> by Jean Liedloff, *Perseus Books* ("A Merloyd Lawrence book") 1975, revised edition 1977, introduction 1985. **The title refers to** Liedloff's idea that humans, like all species, necessarily have built-in expectations and needs—part of a continuum that informs and guides us and which we ignore to our detriment.

http://www.askdrsears.com/ **A terrific site** about attachment parenting and related issues. Dr. and Mrs. Sears have also written many books, which are described at their site.

http://www.attachmentparenting.org/ **Another good site** on attachment parenting.

<u>The Biology of Love</u> by Arthur Janov, *Prometheus Books*, 2000

<u>Why You Get Sick and How You Get Well: The Healing Power of Feelings</u> by Arthur Janov, *Dove Books*, 1996

<u>Prisoners of Pain: Unlocking the Power of the Mind to End Suffering</u> by Arthur Janov, *Anchor/Doubleday*, 1980

http://www.primaltherapy.com/ (Dr. Janov's site)

<u>For Your Own Good: Hidden Cruelty in Child-Rearing and the Roots of Violence</u> by Alice Miller, translation by Hildegarde and Hunter Hannum, *Farrar, Straus, Giroux*, 1983, 1984, 1990

<u>Paths of Life: Seven Scenarios</u> by Alice Miller, *Pantheon Books*, 1998

http://naturalchild.org/ **A site which points out** that children "behave as well as they are treated." Links, children's artwork, "teleclasses," and more. Includes a section on Dr. Miller's work, at *http://naturalchild.org/alice_miller/index.html*.

http://www.alice-miller.com/ (Dr. Miller's own site)

<u>Ghosts from the Nursery: Tracing the Roots of Violence</u> by Robin Karr-Morse and Meredith S. Wiley, *The Atlantic Monthly Press*, 1997

<u>Touching: The Human Significance of the Skin</u> by Ashley Montagu, *Harper & Row*, 1971, 1978, 1986

<u>When Elephants Weep: The Emotional Lives of Animals,</u> by Jeffrey Moussaieff Masson and Susan McCarthy, *Dell Publishing*, 1995. **Dog lovers in particular** will also enjoy Masson's <u>Dogs Never Lie About Love</u>, *Crown Publishers*, 1997.

<u>A General Theory of Love</u> by Thomas Lewis, M.D., Fari Amini, M.D., and Richard Lannon, M.D., *Vintage Books*, 2000

<u>Summerhill: A Radical Approach to Child Rearing</u> by A. S. Neill, *Hart Publishing Co.*, 1960. **No longer in print**, but frequently available in used book stores, and worth seeking out.

<u>The Sudbury Valley School Experience</u>, 3rd edition, by Daniel Greenberg, et. al., *The Sudbury Valley School Press*, 1992

<u>Free at Last: The Sudbury Valley School</u>, 2nd edition, by Daniel Greenberg, *The Sudbury Valley School Press*, 1995.

http://www.sudval.org/ **The website** for the Sudbury Valley School. A web search will bring you other sites related to several schools following the Sudbury model.

<u>Dumbing Us Down: The Hidden Curriculum of Compulsory Schooling</u>, Tenth Anniversary Edition, with a new foreword by Thomas Moore (author of <u>Care of the Soul</u>), by John Taylor Gatto, *New Society Publishers*, 2002

http://www.johntaylorgatto.com/ (John Taylor Gatto's website).

"Public School Pandemonium: My experience as a public school teacher" by Rachel Baxter (now Rachel Kelley), originally published in the *Libertarian Party News* and available on the web at *http://ablechild.org/newsarchive/public_school_pandemonium_ 2 -1-01.htm*

Whatever Happened to Daddy's Little Girl: The Impact of
Fatherlessness on Black Women by Jonetta Rose Barras, *A One World Book*, 2000. **Many of the insights** Ms. Barras conveys apply, I believe, more generally than just to black women who have lost their fathers.

Motherless Daughters: The Legacy of Loss, by Hope Edelman, *Dell Publishing*, 1994. **Another book** more general than its title suggests.

The Alphabet Versus the Goddess: The Conflict Between Word and Image, by Leonard Shlain, *The Penguin Group*, 1998. **Other than tyranny and repressed feeling**, what might oppose the creation of a more free and compassionate world? Shlain makes the case that alphabetic *literacy*, of all things, is an issue we might consider. His thesis is primarily that heavy dependence upon alphabetic literacy ("reading") over-emphasizes the major hemisphere of the brain, causing an imbalance in human life and in society, particularly in regards the treatment of women. The expansion of *image* (photography, television, film, graphic-interface computing, etc.) in modern life will have positive consequences, Shlain believes. See also Shlain's 2003 Sex, Time, and Power.

Wishcraft : How to Get What You Really Want by Barbara Sher with Annie Gottlieb, *Ballantine Books*, 2nd edition, 2003. **What do you** really want out of life? That is an important question, and your answers may reinforce and expand your understanding of what "Paradise" could be.

ON THE NEED FOR FREEDOM AND HUMAN RIGHTS:

Death by Government, by R. J. Rummel, *Transaction Publishers*, 1994

Power Kills: Democracy as a Method of Non-violence by R. J. Rummel, *Transaction Publishers*, 1997

http://www2.hawaii.edu/powerkills/ **Dr. Rummel's site**

http://www.amnesty.org/ **Amnesty International**

The Rape of Nanking: The Forgotten Holocaust of World War II by Iris Chang, *Penguin Books*, 1997

The Black Book of Communism: Crimes, Terror, Repression by Stephane Courtois, et. al, English translation by Jonathan Murphy and Mark Kramer, *Harvard University Press*, 1999

http://www.genocidewatch.org/ **Genocide Watch**, Coordinator for the International Campaign to End Genocide

The Killing Fields (film), starring Sam Waterston, Haing S. Ngor; directed by Roland Joffé, *Warner Studios*, 1984

Tibetan Portrait: The Power of Compassion, photographs by Phil Borges, text by the Dalai Lama, prologue by Jeffrey Hopkins, epilogue by Elie Weisel, *Rizzoli International Publications*, 1996. **This book provides** a brief overview of the on-going devastation wrought by the occupying Red Chinese, while focusing primarily on stunning photographs of Tibetans and short quotations from the Dalai Lama.

The Lord of the Rings trilogy, by J. R. R. Tolkien (many editions; for example, The Hobbit and The Lord of the Rings [boxed set], *Ballantine Books*, 2001). **An epic about a mythical Ring of Power**, which almost no one can resist using, but which leads to horrors even when wielded with the best intentions. The only safe course (and the central theme of the series) is to destroy the Ring completely and forever. The Ring is a remarkable symbol of coercive state power, and the story crafted by J. R. R. Tolkien does it justice—as does the film trilogy directed by Peter Jackson.

"The Unconquered Remnant: The Hopis and Voluntaryism" by Peter Spotswood Dillard. **Dillard provides** an engaging look the Hopi Indians, who ". . . have developed a peaceful, nonviolent, and anarchistic society that has endured for at least a millennium." In other words, the Hopis eschew coercion in favor of cooperation and other non-violent methods; they are voluntaryists. Dillard's article may be found at *http://www. voluntaryist.com/forthcoming/unconquered.php*

The Voluntary City: Choice, Community, and Civil Society, by David T. Beito (Editor), Peter Gordon (Editor), Alexander Tabarrok (Editor), *University of Michigan Press*, 2002. **Despite relentless** propaganda to the contrary, coercive government is not needed for roads, sewers, medical care, charity, police protection, insurance, business regulation, or for anything else. The Voluntary City makes this clear (despite a frequent background assumption that *some* coercive government is necessary) and will be an eye-opener for most readers.

Financial Reckoning Day: Surviving the Soft Depression of the 21st Century, by William Bonner with Addison Wiggin, *John Wiley & Sons, Inc.*, 2003, and Empire of Debt: The Rise Of An Epic Financial Crisis from the same authors and publisher, 2005. **Why such titles here?** Because one of the worst and most fundamental ways that coercive government harms the human condition is *economically*. Bonner and Wiggin provide enough history and fundamentals to make this clear, and to demystify the recent boom/bust cycle besides, including the dot.com crash and other disasters, including some still in progress. Will the coming crash be a "soft depression" or something sharper? Time will tell—if it hasn't already, by the time you read these words.

Economic Freedom of the World, 2005: Annual Report, by James D. Gwartney, *The Cato Institute*, 2005. **Economic freedom** not only creates prosperity: it greatly reduces the risk of war, and is about *50 times* more effective than democracy at reducing violent conflict.

http://www.rsf.org/ **Reporters Without Borders**

ON PARADIGMS, SENSITIVE DEPENDENCE ON EARLY CONDITIONS,
GENETICS, EMERGENCE, AND RELATED MATTERS:

The Structure of Scientific Revolutions, Second Edition, Enlarged, by Thomas S. Kuhn, *University of Chicago Press*, 1962, 1970. **An esoteric work** that nonetheless, indirectly, made "paradigm" a household word.

Nature Via Nurture, by Matt Ridley, *HarperCollins*, 2003. **A riveting look** at the interplay between genetics and environment, with discussions of new research and discovery combined with much detail on the history of related science.

The Blank Slate: The modern denial of human nature, by Steven Pinker, *Penguin Books*, 2002. **In addition to** providing intriguing details about genetic and environmental factors in human life, The Blank Slate documents shocking smear tactics that partisans of both left and right have used against those who point out the obvious: that there *is* a genetically-based human nature. Does acknowledging genetics deny the role of environmental factors? Worse: does it doom us to either fascism or forced collectivism? Of course not.

Complexification: Explaining a Paradoxical World Through the Science of Surprise, by John L. Casti, *HarperPerennial*, 1994. **Casti is prolific;** a search at Amazon.com will bring you several more of his works to choose from, including the classic Paradigms Lost from 1990 and, from 2001, Paradigms Regained.

The Quantum Brain: The Search for Freedom and the Next Generation of Man, by Jeffrey Satinover, *John Wiley and Sons*, 2001. **Includes a spectacularly readable** general description of quantum theory, along with an excellent discussion of how "sensitive dependence" applies to human brains.

Emergence: The Connected Lives of Ants, Brains, Cities, and Software, by Steven Johnson, *Scribner*, 2001. **Johnson's popular and well-written book** remains the best general-audience discussion of emergence that I have seen.

At Home in the Universe: The search for the laws of self-organization and complexity, by Stuart Kauffman, *Oxford University Press*, 1995.

A New Kind of Science, *Wolfram Media, Inc.*, 2002. **More technically-minded readers** may be interested in the writings of Stephen Wolfram, including "Cellular Automata as Models of Complexity", *Nature*, October 1984.

The Tipping Point: How Little Things Can Make a Big Difference by Malcolm Gladwell, *Back Bay Books*, 2002. **Although not explicitly about chaos** or "sensitive dependence on early conditions," The Tipping Point is an excellent discussion of what is sometimes called the butterfly effect, as it relates to social action in human society—and is thus quite relevant to The Paradise Paradigm and to anyone interested in helping to foster positive changes in the world. Gladwell's Blink: The Power of Thinking Without Thinking (*Little, Brown*, 2005) is a worthy companion volume.

APPENDIX TWO

"LOVE ONE ANOTHER"

Even as a tree has a single trunk but many branches and leaves, there is one religion—human religion—but any number of faiths.
— *M. K. Gandhi*

WHAT IS RELIGION? Having "a relationship with God" or otherwise being sincerely religious means, among other things, maintaining a dialog with one's inner truth. Religion gives us a framework within which to acknowledge that we *have* an inner truth and that it is worth listening to.

The most basic element of that truth is the importance of love, as every true religion makes clear.

– *2* –

THE ADMONITION to "love one another"—in those exact words—occurs twelve times in the King James version of the New Testament, and many more times in slightly different wording. (The *Project Gutenberg* **Etext** of <u>The King James Bible</u> was used for this count).

Of course, Christianity is not the only religion that counsels love: for example, the Jain, Buddhist, and Hindu religions all center, to one

extent or another, on compassion and the concept of "ahimsa"—
non-violence to all living things.

Consider these words from Chapter 16 of the <u>Bhagavad-Gita</u>, as
translated by Sir Edwin Arnold (1885)—here the Lord is speaking to
the mortal Arjuna about the characteristics of those whose path is
divine:

> . . . humbleness,
> Uprightness, heed to injure nought which lives,
> Truthfulness, slowness unto wrath. . . and charity
> Which spieth no man's faults; and tenderness
> Towards all that suffer . . .

More "tenderness towards all that suffer" would, by itself, go a
long way toward improving the world, would it not?

– 3 –

THE FOCUS ON LOVE AND COMPASSION clearly exists in other religions as well—some would say it is a *defining characteristic* of any
true religion *per se.*

For example, the passages extolling love in the New Testament
are worth reading regardless of one's religious beliefs. In particular,
it should be noted that *this is not a supernatural or specifically religious exhortation.* While supernatural elements (of a God in
Heaven and of an afterlife, especially) exist in Christian writing,
and while these elements do not fit well with modern tastes and
with the scientific mind-set, the Christian exhortation to love one
another is *clearly meant to encourage real people, here in the daily
world, to feel and to express more love for one another; it is an apparently heart-felt cry for more love in the world.*

For example, from *The Gospel According to Saint John*, quoting
Jesus:

13:34 A new commandment I give unto you, That ye love one another; as I have loved you, that ye also love one another.

13:35 By this shall all men know that ye are my disciples, if ye have love one to another.

A pause here; please reflect for a moment on those two verses. They are among the clearest and most direct statements from Jesus' own mouth (as reported by the disciple John, in this case) that we have.

How are we to know if someone is a Christian?

Simple: Jesus says you are is His disciple if you ". . . have love one to another." *That* is how we can tell if someone is truly a Christian.

Another example (although not quoting Jesus), from *The First Epistle General of John*:

4:12 No man hath seen God at any time. If we love one another, God dwelleth in us, and his love is perfected in us.

Three more verses (again not quoting Jesus' own words), these from *The Epistle of Paul the Apostle to the Romans*:

13:8 Owe no man any thing, but to love one another: for he that loveth another hath fulfilled the law.

13:9 For this, Thou shalt not commit adultery, Thou shalt not kill, Thou shalt not steal, Thou shalt not bear false witness, Thou shalt not covet; and if there be any other commandment, it is briefly comprehended in this saying, namely, Thou shalt love thy neighbour as thyself.

13:10 Love worketh no ill to his neighbour: therefore love is the fulfilling of the law.

Where do children fit into all this? As you might expect, they have a special place. From *The Gospel According to Saint Mark*:

> 10:13: And they brought young children to him, that he should touch them: and his disciples rebuked those that brought them.

> 10:14: But when Jesus saw it, he was much displeased, and said unto them, Suffer the little children to come unto me, and forbid them not: for of such is the kingdom of God.

> 10:15: Verily I say unto you, Whosoever shall not receive the kingdom of God as a little child, he shall not enter therein.

These passages from the New Testament—about love and about children—amount to an open war on neurosis. They suggest that one way to see the kingdom of heaven is as an emotionally healthy world, *here on Earth*. Jesus makes this point very directly in a well-known passage in *Luke*:

> 17:21 Neither shall they say, Lo here! or, lo there! for, behold, the kingdom of God is within you.*

Surely, whether a supernatural heaven and an afterlife exist or not, much of Jesus' teaching was specifically aimed at bringing more love to the everyday world of the here-and-now, and to protecting children as a necessary part of that.

From *The Gospel According to Saint Matthew*:

> 18:1 At the same time came the disciples unto Jesus, saying, Who is the greatest in the kingdom of heaven?

---

* This calls to mind the traditional Indian greeting of namaste: "I bow to the divine within you." The greeting goes with a gesture: hands pressed together in front of one's chest, and a subtle bow of the head and shoulders.

18:2 And Jesus called a little child unto him, and set him in the midst of them,

18:3 And said, Verily I say unto you, Except ye be converted, and become as little children, ye shall not enter into the kingdom of heaven.

This suggests an interesting way to judge psychotherapy: does it help the patients to "become as little children?" That is, does it help them to be more open to their feelings (as children are) and to be more real, less cynical, more loving?

Certainly, this is an *important* way to judge any Christian sect: does it promote love, does it, in a real and practical sense, help protect the young and to provide for them the love necessary to grow into loving adults? Does the sect produce adults who are open to their feelings, and without guile or hatred? Does it produce adults who are "as little children?" If not, can it truly be called "Christian?"

It is worth observing that despite such clear language about love, and despite the compassion shown by many Christians, *some* Christians are anything but loving in their behavior. (The same can be said about members of any large group, of course). This highlights an important truth: people observe and practice their religion, along with everything else they do, in accordance with their state of emotional health.

PRIMAL THEORY

PRIMAL THEORY DESERVES particular mention here because in matters of feeling, at least, the Primal viewpoint is in large measure the viewpoint of this book.

Primal Theory grew out of psychologist Arthur Janov's experience in clinical practice. In the late 1960s, that practice evolved into what he called Primal Therapy.

In patient after patient, Dr. Janov found that the underlying causes of neurotic symptoms were traumatic events from the patient's early life. In The Primal Scream, published in 1970, he describes neurosis this way:

Neurosis is a disease of feeling. At its core is the suppression of feeling and its transmutation into a wide range of neurotic behavior.

The dazzling variety of neurotic symptoms from insomnia to sexual perversion have caused us to think of neurosis in categories. But different symptoms are not distinct disease entities; all neuroses stem from the same specific cause and respond to the same specific treatment. [p. 20]

Furthermore, the brain deals with both *physical* and *psychological* pain in a similar fashion. For example, a 2003 study reported in the journal *Science* found that social rejection and physical pain both caused activity in the same brain region—the anterior cingulate cortex—and that subjects reporting the most distress showed the highest levels of activity in that region.[44]

There are other reasons to believe that on many levels, pain is processed much the same whether it is "social" or "physical." In other words: pain is pain, regardless of the source.

– 2 –

WHY NEUROSIS DOES NOT HEAL SPONTANEOUSLY

Traumatic levels of pain from early in life never get fully experienced in the normal course of events. Full experience of trauma is blocked by the mechanisms of repression in the brain and body. The traumatic experience remains trapped in the system, *still on its way to consciousness.*

Blocking the experience from consciousness is a constant and lifelong job, visible in the symptoms conventionally termed "neurosis" as well as in other behavior (slightly elevated blood pressure and temperature, for example—which Primal Therapy reduces in many patients).[45]

This is why it is so hard for people to change in fundamental, real ways. People can exchange symptoms—stop smoking and take up something else, for instance (even if the "something else" is only overeating or higher blood pressure)—but the energy driving the symptom never leaves us, until we feel and *connect* the experience of repressed events that are causing the tension and symptoms in the first place.

Most people never do that, of course: they live their entire adulthood repressing all of their childhood traumas. (So again: less early pain makes for a better life). This is why people in their sixties, seventies, and beyond are *still* neurotic. They don't get better, because "getting better" requires feeling old pain.

Repressed experience becomes—instead of a simple memory—a lifelong force, an experience frozen in time, waiting patiently and insistently to be felt, but eternally rebuffed from full consciousness.

– 3 –

BECAUSE THE IMPULSE TO AVOID PAIN is so fundamental to life, it is no surprise that people want a painless way to get well. For the most part, in fact, they don't think they *need* to get well; they want a quick fix of some sort to feel better. People want a new car, a new lover, a cigarette, a snack from the kitchen, a pill—anything. Who could blame them? "Painless" is what we are programmed to want, right down to our DNA.

That is the main reason why *prevention* of the pain that causes neurosis is the only solution to the problems of the human condition. Fixing emotional damage from early in life is difficult, and few people are interested in even beginning the process of healing.

Primal Theory predicts that prevention of emotional damage will prevent neurosis—and, by extension, that reducing emotional damage world-wide will improve the human condition, globally.

That, as you will already understand, is exactly the prediction—and the purpose—of the Paradise Paradigm and of this book.

17,421 EXAMPLES OF "SENSITIVE DEPENDENCE ON EARLY CONDITIONS"

An Introduction to "Turning Gold into Lead"

IN 2001, the *Journal of the American Medical Association* published a review of the literature which found over fifty studies showing that repeated childhood abuse had "numerous sequelae" in later life, including greatly increased risk for suicidality, depression, and post traumatic stress syndrome.*

Despite such evidence, few appreciate the power that early life has in shaping later life. Risks for *cancer* and *heart disease*, for example, are several times higher for adults who suffered frequent and severe abuse or distress in childhood. Adult behavior, adult emotional health, and *adult experience itself* are also affected by experiences in childhood.

When a study finds that abused children have more problems later in life, it is "less-abused children" that this increase is in relation

---

* "Psychiatrists Explore Legacy of Traumatic Stress in Early Life" by Lynne Lamberg, *JAMA*, August 1, 2001

to. That is to say, such a study is also showing that *loving and appropriate* childhood experience is highly protective against emotional and physical ill-health, or against violent behavior, or against whatever negative outcome the study found associated with the abuse (or other distress) being looked at. Positive childhoods yield positive outcomes in adulthood; negative childhoods yield negative outcomes.

The single most compelling study on this topic may be the Adverse Childhood Experiences (ACE) Study, which uses data from over 17,000 volunteers and has been the subject of numerous articles in professional journals (see references at end of article below). As this book goes to press, the ACE Study is nearing its ten-year milestone and new articles on the study will soon be published.

Dr. Vincent J. Felitti, co-designer of the ACE Study, has generously offered an article—"The Relationship of Adverse Childhood Experiences to Adult Health: Turning Gold Into Lead"—to be reprinted here in its entirety. His article contains both surprising information and unusual insight.

I have emphasized in this book that "prevention is the only long-term solution." Dr. Felitti's article makes clear not only the need for prevention of abuse and distress in childhood but also, indirectly, the staggering power we have to improve the human condition itself—individually, and eventually world-wide—by simply improving our treatment of the young.

THE RELATIONSHIP OF ADVERSE CHILDHOOD EXPERIENCES TO ADULT HEALTH: TURNING GOLD INTO LEAD*

Vincent J. Felitti, MD
Kaiser Permanente Medical Care Program
7060 Clairemont Mesa Boulevard
San Diego, California   92111

VJFMDSDCA@msn.com

THE QUESTION of what determines adult health and well-being is important to all countries. The Adverse Childhood Experiences (ACE) Study[1] is a major American research project that poses the question of whether, and how, childhood experiences affect adult health decades later. This question is being answered with the ongoing collaboration of Robert Anda, MD at the Centers for Disease Control (CDC) and the cooperation of 17,421 adults at Kaiser Permanente's Department of Preventive Medicine in San Diego, California. Kaiser Permanente is a multispecialty, prepaid, private health insurance system or Health Maintenance Organization [HMO]. The findings from the ACE Study provide a remarkable insight into how we become what we are as individuals and as a nation. They are important medically, socially, and economically[2]. Indeed, they have given us reason to reconsider the very structure of primary care medical practice in America.

The ACE Study reveals a powerful relationship between our emotional experiences as children and our physical and mental

---

* English translation of: Felitti VJ. Belastungen in der Kindheit und Gesundheit im Erwachsenenalter: die Verwandlung von Gold in Blei. Z psychsom Med Psychother 2002; 48(4): 359-369.

health as adults, as well as the major causes of adult mortality in the United States. It documents the conversion of traumatic emotional experiences in childhood into organic disease later in life. How does this happen, this reverse alchemy, turning the gold of a new-born infant into the lead of a depressed, diseased adult? The Study makes it clear that time does not *heal* some of the adverse experiences we found so common in the childhoods of a large population of middle-aged, middle class Americans. One does not 'just get over' some things, not even fifty years later[3].

The Adverse Childhood Experiences Study is an outgrowth of observations we made in the mid 1980s in an obesity program that had a high dropout rate. The first of many unexpected discoveries was that the majority of the dropouts actually were successfully losing weight. Accidentally and to our surprise, we learned from detailed life interviews of 286 such individuals that childhood sexual abuse was remarkably common and, if present, always ante-dated the onset of their obesity. No one previously had sought this kind of medical information from them but many patients spoke of their conscious awareness of an association between abuse and obesity. Some told of instances where they had brought up their history of abuse only to have the information rejected by a physician as being in the distant past and hence of no relevance to current problems.

The counterintuitive aspect was that, for many people, obesity was not their problem; it was their protective *solution* to problems that previously had never been acknowledged to anyone. An early insight was the remark of a woman who was raped at age twenty-three and gained 105 pounds in the year subsequent: "Overweight is overlooked and that's the way I need to be." The contrast was striking between this statement and her desire to lose weight. Similarly, two men who were guards at the State Penitentiary became anxious after each losing over one hundred pounds. They said that they felt much safer going to work looking larger than life rather than normal size. In general, we found the simultaneous presence of strong opposing forces to be common in our obese patients. Many were driving with one foot on the brakes and one on the gas, wanting to lose weight but fearful of the change in social and sexual expectations that would be brought about by major weight loss.

Researchers at the Centers for Disease Control (CDC) recognized the importance of these clinical observations and helped design a large, epidemiologically sound study that would provide definitive proof of our findings and of their significance. The Adverse Childhood Experiences Study was carried out in Kaiser Permanente's Department of Preventive Medicine in San Diego. This was an ideal setting because for many years we had carried out detailed biomedical, psychological, and social (biopsychosocial) evaluations of over 58,000 adult Kaiser Health Plan members a year. Moreover, the patients were from a typical middle class American population. We asked 26,000 consecutive adults coming through the Department if they would be interested in helping us understand how childhood events might affect adult health status. Seventy-one percent agreed.

We asked these volunteers to help us study eight categories of childhood abuse and household dysfunction. The abuse categories were: recurrent physical abuse, recurrent severe emotional abuse, and contact sexual abuse. The five categories of household dysfunction were: growing up in a household where someone was in prison; where the mother was treated violently; with an alcoholic or a drug user; where someone was chronically depressed, mentally ill, or suicidal; and where at least one biological parent was lost to the patient during childhood—regardless of cause. An individual exposed to none of the categories had an ACE Score of 0; an individual exposed to any four had an ACE Score of 4, etc. In addition, a prospective arm of the Study is following the cohort for at least 5 years to compare distant childhood experiences against current Emergency Department use, doctor office visits, medication costs, hospitalization, and death.

Dr. Anda, my co-principal investigator at CDC, designed with great skill the massive data management and retrospective and prospective components of the Study. Because the average participant was 57 years old, we actually were measuring the effect of childhood experiences on adult health status a half-century later. The full text of our initial report is at *http://www.meddevel.com/site.mash?left=/ library.exe&m1=4&m2=1&right=/library.exe&action=search_form&s earch.mode=simple&site=AJPM&jcode=AMEPRE*

Our two most important findings are that these adverse childhood experiences:

- are vastly more common than recognized or acknowledged and
- have a powerful relation to adult health a half-century later.

This combination makes them important to the nation's health and to medical practice. Slightly more than half of our middle-class population of Kaiser members experienced one or more of the categories of adverse childhood experience that we studied. One in four were exposed to two categories of adverse experience; one in 16 were exposed to four categories. Given an exposure to one category, there is 80% likelihood of exposure to another category. Of course, all this is well shielded by social taboos against seeking or obtaining this kind of information. Furthermore, one may miss the forest for the trees if one studies the categories individually. They do not occur in isolation; for instance, a child does not grow up with an alcoholic parent or with domestic violence in an otherwise supportive and well-functioning household. The question to ask is: How will these childhood experiences play out decades later in a doctor's office? To study that, we will categorize outcomes into organic disease and emotional disorder.

ORGANIC DISEASE:

We shall first look at the relationship of adverse childhood experiences to smoking[4]. Smoking underlies some of the most important causes of death in America; there has been a strong public health effort to eradicate smoking in California. In spite of initial success in significantly reducing the number of smokers, there has been no further net decrease in recent years although the efforts against smoking have continued. Because of this, smoking in the face of California's strong social pressures against it is often attributed to 'addiction'. The usual concept of tobacco addiction implies that it is attributable to characteristics that are intrinsic within the molecular structure of nicotine. However, we found that the higher the ACE Score, the greater the likelihood of current smoking. In other words, current smoking is strongly related in a progressive dose-response manner to what happened decades ago in childhood. Finding 'addiction' attributable to characteristics that are intrinsic in early life experiences challenges the conventional concept of addiction. The psychoactive benefits of nicotine are well established in the medical literature although they are little remembered. Are smoking and its related diseases the result of self-treatment of concealed problems that occurred in childhood?

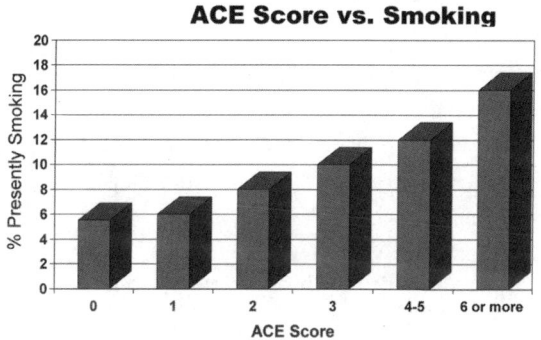

Chronic obstructive pulmonary disease (COPD) also has a strong relationship to the ACE Score, as does the early onset of regular smoking. A person with an ACE Score of 4 is 260% more likely to have COPD than is a person with an ACE Score of 0. This relationship has the same graded, dose-response effect that is present for all the associations we found. Moreover, all the relationships presented here have a p value of .001 or stronger.

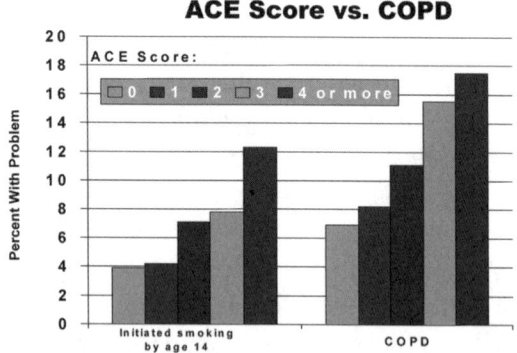

When we compared hepatitis in ACE Score 0 patients with hepatitis in ACE Score 4 patients, there was a 240% increase in prevalence. A progressive dose response effect was present with every increase in the ACE Score. Similarly, with regard to sexually transmitted disease, comparison of the adjusted odds ratio for sexually transmitted disease in these same two groups showed a 250% increase at ACE Score 4 compared to ACE Score 0.

In the United States, intravenous drug use is a major public health problem with which little progress has been made. It is widely recognized as a cause of several life-threatening diseases. We found that the relationship of iv drug use to adverse childhood experiences is powerful and graded at every step; it provides a perfect dose-response curve.

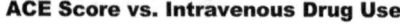

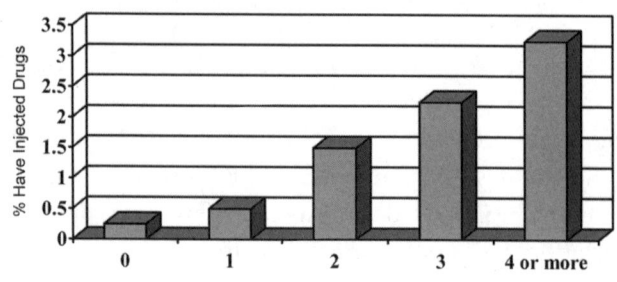

In Epidemiology, these results are almost unique in their magnitude. For example, a male child with an ACE Score of 6 has a 4,600% increase in the likelihood of later becoming an iv drug user when compared to a male child with an ACE Score of 0. Since no one injects heroin to get endocarditis or AIDS, why *is* it used? Might heroin be used for the relief of profound anguish dating back to childhood experiences? Might its psychoactive effects be the best coping device that an individual can find? Is intravenous drug use properly viewed as a personal *solution* to problems that are well concealed by social niceties and taboo? If so, is intravenous drug use a public health problem or a personal solution? Is it both? How often are public health problems personal solutions? Is drug abuse self-destructive or is it a desperate attempt at self-healing, albeit while accepting a significant future risk? This is an important point because primary prevention is far more difficult than anticipated. Is this because non-recognition of the *benefits* of health risk behaviors leads them to be viewed as irrational and as solely having damaging consequences? Does this major oversight leave us speaking in platitudes instead of understanding the causal basis of some of our intractable public health problems?

EMOTIONAL DISORDERS:
When we looked at purely emotional outcomes like self-defined current depression or self-reported suicide attempts, we find equally powerful effects. For instance, we found that an individual with an ACE Score of 4 or more was 460% more likely to be suffering from depression than an individual with an ACE Score of 0. Should one doubt the reliability of this, we found that there was a 1,220% increase in attempted suicide between these two groups. At higher ACE Scores, the prevalence of attempted suicide increases 30-51fold (3,000-5,100%)! Our article describing this staggering effect was published in a recent issue of the Journal of the American Medical Association[5]. Overall, using the technique of population attributable risk, we found that between two-thirds and 80% of

all attempted suicides could be attributed to adverse childhood experiences.

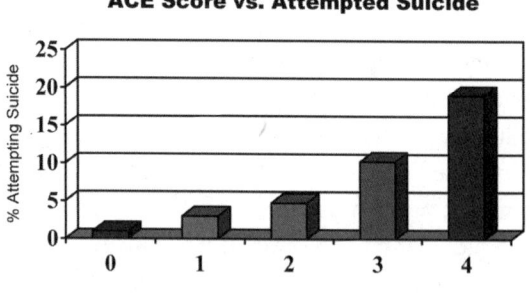

ACE Score vs. Attempted Suicide

% Attempting Suicide

ACE Score

In addition to these examples, we found many other measures of adult health have a strong, graded relationship to what happened in childhood: heart disease, fractures, diabetes, obesity, unintended pregnancy[6], sexually transmitted diseases[7], and alcoholism were more frequent. Occupational health and job performance worsened progressively as the ACE Score increased. Some of these results are yet to be published, as is all the data from the prospective arm of the Study that will relate adverse childhood experiences to medical care costs, disease, and death a half-century later.

Clearly, we have shown that adverse childhood experiences are common, destructive, and have an effect that often lasts for a lifetime. They are the most important determinant of the health and well-being of our nation. Unfortunately, these problems are painful to recognize and difficult to deal with. Most physicians would far rather deal with traditional organic disease. Certainly, it is easier to do so, but that approach also leads to troubling treatment failures and the frustration of expensive diagnostic quandaries where everything is ruled out but nothing is ruled in.

Our usual approach to many adult chronic diseases reminds one of the relationship of smoke to fire. For a person unfamiliar with fires, it would initially be tempting to treat the smoke because that is the most visible aspect of the problem. Fortunately, fire departments learned long ago to distinguish cause from effect; else, they would carry fans rather than water hoses to their work. What we have learned in the ACE Study represents the underlying fire in medical practice where we often treat symptoms rather than underlying causes.

If the treatment implications of what we found in the ACE Study are far-reaching, the prevention aspects are positively daunting. The very nature of the material is such as to make one uncomfortable. Why would one want to leave the relative comfort of traditional organic disease and enter this area of threatening uncertainty that none of us has been trained to deal with? And yet, literally as I am writing these words, I am interrupted to consult on a 70-year-old woman who is diabetic and hypertensive. The initial description given to me left out the fact that she is morbidly obese (one doesn't go out of one's way to identify what one can't handle). Review of her chart shows her to be chronically depressed, never married, and, because we routinely ask the question of 58,000 adults a year, to have been raped by her older brother six decades ago when she was ten. That brother molested her sister who is said also to be leading a troubled life.

We found that 22% of our Kaiser members were sexually abused as children. How does that affect a person later in life? How does it show up in the doctor's office? What does it mean that sexual abuse is never spoken of? Most of us initially are uncomfortable about obtaining or using such information; therefore we find it useful routinely to pose such questions to all patients by questionnaire. Our Yes response rates are quite high as the ACE Study indicates. We then ask patients acknowledging such experience, *"How did that affect you later in life?"* This question is easy to ask and is neither judgmental nor threatening to hear. It works well and you should remember to use it. It typically provides profoundly important information, and does so concisely. It often gives one a clear idea where to go with treatment.

What then is this woman's diagnosis? Is she just another hyper-tensive, diabetic old woman or is there more to the practice of medicine? Here is the way we conceptualized her problems:

Childhood sexual abuse
Chronic depression
Morbid obesity
Diabetes mellitus
Hypertension
Hyperlipidemia
Coronary artery disease
Macular degeneration
Psoriasis

This is not a comfortable diagnostic formulation because it points out that our attention is typically focused on tertiary consequences, far downstream. It reveals that the primary issues are well protected by social convention and taboo. It points out that we physicians have limited ourselves to the smallest part of the problem, that part where we are comfortable as mere prescribers of medication. Which diagnostic choice shall we make? Who shall make it? And, if not now, when?

References:

1. Felitti VJ, Anda RF, Nordenberg D, Williamson DF, Spitz AM, Edwards V, Koss MP, et al JS. The rela-tionship of adult health status to childhood abuse and household dysfunction. American Journal of Preventive Medicine. 1998;14:245-258.

2. Foege WH. Adverse childhood experiences: A public health perspective (editorial). American Journal of Preventive Medicine. 1998;14:354-355.

3. Weiss JS, Wagner SH. What explains the negative consequences of adverse childhood experiences on adult health? Insights from cognitive and neuroscience research (editorial). American Journal of Preventive Medicine. 1998;14:356-360.

4. Anda RF, Croft JB, Felitti VJ, Nordenberg D, Giles WH, Williamson DF, et al. Adverse childhood expe-riences and smoking during adolescence and adulthood. Journal of the American Medical Association. 1999;282:1652-1658.

5. Dube SR, Anda RF, Felitti VJ, Chapman DP, Williamson DF, Giles WH. Childhood Abuse, Household Dysfunction, and the Risk of Attempted Suicide Throughout the Lifespan. JAMA 2001; 286: 3089-3096.

6. Dietz PM, Spitz AM, Anda RF, et al. Unintended pregnancy among adult women exposed to abuse or household dysfunction during their childhood. Journal of the American Medical Association. 1999;282:1359-1364.

7. Hillis SD, Anda RF, Felitti VJ, Nordenberg D, Marchbanks PA. Adverse childhood experiences and sexu-ally transmitted diseases in men and women: a retrospective study. Pediatrics 2000 106(1):E11.

ACKNOWLEDGEMENTS

MANY PEOPLE HELPED MAKE THIS BOOK better than it otherwise would have been. I am particularly grateful to those who provided early feedback and commentary, including Manjula Jain, Amy Lawrence, Carol Mathews, Rob Moody, Joy Butler, Andrew Allport, Manfred Bauer, and Rachel Kelley.

Thanks also to those at the Thoreau-inspired *www.strike-the-root.com* ("There are a thousand hacking at the branches of evil to one who is striking at the root."). Portions of this book have been published, in slightly different form, in columns at Strike-The-Root.

Parts of Chapter Six were published, again in slightly different form, in the *Libertarian Party News* (*www.lp.org/*). Special thanks to Bill Winters for his assistance and encouragement.

My thanks to Arthur Janov, Ph.D. for generously allowing brief quotations from a wide range of his writings, including <u>The Primal Scream</u>, <u>The Feeling Child</u>, <u>Imprints: The Lifelong Effects of the Birth Experience</u>, and <u>The Biology of Love</u>.

Martha Sears, RN and Dr. William Sears were kind enough to offer permission for use of brief material about Attachment Parenting from their website, *http://www.askdrsears.com/*.

My thanks to Jean Liedloff for permission to use a quote from <u>The Continuum Concept: In Search of Happiness Lost</u>, *Perseus Books*, revised edition 1977.

I am also grateful for permission to use the brief quote from Martin H. Teicher's "Scars That Won't Heal: The neurobiology of child abuse," *Scientific American*, March 2002.

My thanks to Dr. John L. Casti for permission to use a short quotation from his <u>Complexification: Explaining a paradoxical world through the science of surprise</u>, *HarperPerennial*, 1994.

Donald W. Miller, Jr., M.D., was kind enough to check the manuscript for medical and scientific errors. Any that remain are my own, and indeed some changes and additions have been made to the text since Dr. Miller saw it.

Thanks to author and playwright Karen Sunde for permission to use the evocative quotation at the top of Chapter Six—"To love is to receive a glimpse of heaven." The quote is from Sunde's play <u>Kabuki Othello</u>, first produced in 1986.

Thanks to Vincent J. Felitti, M.D., for graciously offering an English translation of his complete article "The Relationship of Adverse Childhood Experiences to Adult Health: Turning gold into lead" from *Z psychsom Med Psychother*, (2002, no copyright), and of related material. The study he writes about (and which he co-designed) is a landmark, and I very much appreciate being able to include this well-written piece here as an Appendix.

John Langdon created the "Love and Freedom" logo seen at the end of Chapter 6. More of his work may be found at *www. johnlangdon.net/*.

Shannon Bodie at the graphics house Lightbourne (*www.light bourne.com/*) created the attractive designs for both the cover and the book interior, and handled my incessant tinkering with grace and good humor.

Dr. Jan Tyler, Ph.D., provided a detailed copy edit of the manuscript along with useful commentary. Brookes Nohlgren also helped with copy editing. Many changes to the text have been made since then, and in any case whatever unconventional usage and other *faux pas* may remain are my choices, not theirs.

Ellen Reid helped with publishing industry details, as did Dan Poynter through his books and website.

The style of the opening paragraph in Chapter One was suggested to me by Julian Jaynes' <u>The Origin of Consciousness in the</u>

Breakdown of the Bicameral Mind, *Haughton Mifflin Company*, Boston, © 1976, 1990.

The Friedrich Nietzsche quotation used in Chapter Seven is from the excellent Walter Kaufmann translation of the second edition of The Gay Science, 1887, *Random House* (Vintage Books edition), 1974.

Lastly, my wife, Karen, provided careful copy editing, gave useful feedback and commentary on the manuscript, and helped me settle on the title. Despite the book's modest page count, this was a lengthy project—I conceived the idea and began writing the book in 1993—and throughout this long gestation period, I was fortunate to have Karen's love, laughter, and steady enthusiasm for what often seemed an impossibly quixotic undertaking.

NOTES

1. The quote is from William Wordsworth's <u>The Rainbow</u>, published in (or near, depending on source) 1802.

2. <u>The Structure of Scientific Revolutions</u>, Second Edition, Enlarged, by Thomas S. Kuhn, *University of Chicago Press*, 1962, 1970. On the famous difficulty of pinning down a precise definition of the word: In the Postscript to the Second Edition, on page 175, Kuhn acknowledges that his book uses "paradigm" with at least two different definitions. Later, on page 181, he goes so far as to say that his "original text leaves no more obscure or important question" than the definition of that central term. Kuhn then graciously shares with us that a reader had found *twenty-two different ways* "paradigm" is used in the first edition.

3. "Achievements in Public Health, 1900-1999: Control of Infectious Diseases" at the U.S. Centers for Disease Control
   http://www.cdc.gov/epo/mmwr/preview/mmwrhtml/mm4829a1.htm
   An excerpt:

   > Deaths from infectious diseases have declined markedly in the United States during the 20th century (Figure 1). This decline contributed to a sharp drop in infant and child mortality (1, 2) and to the 29.2-year increase in life expectancy (2). In 1900, 30.4% of all deaths occurred among children aged less than 5 years; in 1997, that percentage was only 1.4%. In 1900, the three leading causes of death were pneumonia, tuberculosis (TB), and diarrhea and enteritis, which (together with diphtheria) caused one third of all deaths (Figure 2). Of

these deaths, 40% were among children aged less than 5 years (1). In 1997, heart disease and cancers accounted for 54.7% of all deaths, with 4.5% attributable to pneumonia, influenza, and human immunodeficiency virus (HIV) infection (2). Despite this overall progress, one of the most devastating epidemics in human history occurred during the 20th century: the 1918 influenza pandemic that resulted in 20 million deaths, including 500,000 in the United States, in less than 1 year—more than have died in as short a time during any war or famine in the world (3). HIV infection, first recognized in 1981, has caused a pandemic that is still in progress, affecting 33 million people and causing an estimated 13.9 million deaths (4). These episodes illustrate the volatility of infectious disease death rates and the unpredictability of disease emergence.

Also:
    "Ten Great Public Health Achievements—United States, 1900—1999" in the CDC's *Morbidity and Mortality Weekly Report*, April 2, 1999 at *http://www.cdc.gov/mmwr/PDF/wk/mm4812.pdf*
    This document includes charts, tables, and a good, readable summary of how dramatic the improvement in our control of infectious disease really is.

4. Related topics include self-organization, complex systems, chaos, and cellular automata. Writings on these topics are not all in agreement about the *relationship* of these concepts; for instance, "emergence" is sometimes described as merely the end-point of "self-organization" and by other authors as *itself* a principle of self-organization. There are many discussions of *emergence* in print, but I was moved to include the topic in this chapter after reading Steven Johnson's <u>Emergence: The Connected Lives of Ants, Brains, Cities, and Software</u>, *Scribner*, 2001.

5. "Chaotic" does not mean "random." John L. Casti describes the distinction as follows in <u>Complexification: Explaining a paradoxical world through the science of surprise</u>, *HarperPerennial*, 1994 (p. 103):

    Chaos involves a deterministic mechanism that generates the *appearance* of randomness; a genuine random process has no such deterministic underpinning.

Casti also makes the point that "… systems with strange attractors are the rule, not the exception. So if you're dealing with mathematical representations of the real world, then you're dealing with strange attractors, or, in the vernacular, chaos." (p. 37)

6. Chapter 5 and Appendix 3: *Primal Theory* in this book, and the works of Dr. Arthur Janov in the "Further Reading" section, provide further details. While a few symptoms may be caused strictly by physical problems, in most cases even where a physical problem (the wrong level of a chemical or hormone, for example) can be identified, the *cause* of that physical problem is, at least in part, repressed feeling. The exact percentage of neurotic symptoms due to old, repressed pain is not important to our thesis; the vast majority certainly are. The comment about the amount spent, world-wide, on drugs, is from The Underground Empire: Where Crime and Governments Embrace, by James Mills, 1986. In the same paragraph, the phrase "the lifetime sentence" is a paraphrase of the first section subheading in Dr. Arthur Janov's Prisoners of Pain, 1980. Those three words also show up on page 9 of his Why You Get Sick and How You Get Well, *Dove Books*, 1996.

7. This paradigm shift almost certainly happened long before the 1400s, at least among the intelligencia, despite the entrenched idea that Columbus' contemporaries were flat-Earthers (see, for instance, Inventing the Flat Earth: Columbus and modern historians by Jeffrey Burton Russell, 1997). My thanks to James Hannam at *http://www. bede.org.uk/* for bringing this to my attention. The late Isaac Asimov backed the view that Columbus' contemporaries knew the Earth was a sphere, although they had the size wrong, at about 18,000 miles circumference instead of roughly 24,000 miles. In any case, the average person-on-the-street probably held different views from those of the highly educated, just as many Americans today dismiss Darwinism despite that theory's overwhelming acceptance among the scientific community.

8. The actual landfalls made by Columbus during his four voyages to the New World remain a matter of dispute; Cuba is widely thought to be among the landfalls made during his first and second voyages.

9. The Feeling Child by Arthur Janov, Ph.D., *Simon and Schuster*, 1973, p. 144.

10. For example, "Illicit Psychoactive Substance Use, Heavy Use, Abuse, and Dependence in a US Population-Based Sample of Male Twins," Kenneth S. Kendler, MD; Laura M. Karkowski, PhD; Michael C. Neale, PhD; Carol A. Prescott, PhD, *Arch Gen Psychiatry,* 2000; 57:261-269. In short: yes, genetics plays a role in emotional health, as it does in everything from sports ability to food preference; some people are more susceptible to drug abuse or depression, for instance. But these people are not fated to be drug abusers or depressives; they are merely more sensitive in particular ways, and for them, it is even more critical that early experience be non-traumatic.

11. *New Scientist* magazine, 4/1/2000, "Nurture compounds nature in early arrivals."

12. "The Contribution of Mild and Moderate Preterm Birth to Infant Mortality" by Michael S. Kramer, MD, et. al., *Journal of the American Medical Association,* August 16, 2000 *http://jama.ama-assn.org/issues/ v284n7/abs/joc00258.html*

13. "Gum disease linked to premature birth," by John Tuohy, *USA Today,* May 8, 2000

14. Many psychologists and others have pointed this out; it is certainly not a new idea. Arthur Janov is particularly good at describing what neurosis is and how it is transmitted from generation to generation. The "Further Reading" section includes a partial list of Dr. Janov's work. But again, many others have put forth the basic idea that traumatic feelings are repressed in childhood and that this condition (neurosis) is passed from generation to generation.

15. One exception The Quantum Brain: the search for freedom and the next generation of man by Jeffrey Satinover, *John Wiley & Sons,* 2001.

16. "Pain in newborns may lower threshold later" by Paul Recer, *Associated Press,* as printed in the *San Diego Union Tribune,* July 27, 2000.

17. "Breast cancer and breast-feeding: collaborative reanalysis of individual data from 47 epidemiological studies in 30 countries, including 50,302 women with breast cancer and 96,973 women without the disease" by Prof. Valerie Beral in *Lancet* 2002; 360: 187-95

18. "Breast-feeding lifts the spirits of new mothers" by Marilyn Elias, *USA Today,* 3/17/2002

19. One good overview of this topic is <u>Ghosts From the Nursery: Tracing the Roots of Violence</u> by Robin Karr-Morse and Meredith S. Wiley, *The Atlantic Monthly Press*, 1997. The Introduction by Dr. T. Berry Brazelton includes this summary statement: "Story after story points to the importance of intrauterine conditions and early experiences which can lead to future violent behavior."

20. *British Medical Journal* 2002; 324:26-27, as reported at *http://www.reutershealth.com* for January 4, 2002.

21. <u>Ghosts From the Nursery</u>, p. 70

22. "Prenatal stress may cause disorder," by Rogers Worthington, Chicago Tribune (as reprinted in the *San Diego Union-Tribune*), 2/2/94.

23. "Violence-prone men may be both born and made," by Tim Friend, *USA Today*, February 14, 1994

24. Personal correspondence

25. <u>The Gay Science</u> by Friedrich Nietzsche, 1887, as translated by Walter Kaufmann, *Random House* (Vintage Books edition), 1974

26. It is more accurate to say that emotional damage from childhood never heals *unless* it is felt and connected fully and consciously. To re-live a traumatic event—this time with full consciousness—is to convert it from a painful trauma *still waiting to happen* into nothing more than another old memory, albeit an unpleasant one. The difference is that while unfelt, the repressed trauma exerts a continuous pressure; it literally *has not fully happened yet*, and the body and mind are in a state of tension, waiting for the event and feeling to finish and defending against what is coming. Complicating the issue is that physical changes in the brain are caused by early abuse or other trauma, and some of these changes may be irreversible, regardless of the amount or type of therapy. Those interested in more detail are referred to the works of Dr. Arthur Janov in the "Further Reading" section.

27. The AA website, *http://www.aa.org/em24doc6.html*, asserts that "...all available medical testimony indicates that alcoholism is a progressive illness, that it cannot be cured in the ordinary sense of the term, but that it can be arrested through total abstinence from alcohol in any form."

28. "Children of the Garden Island," Emmy Werner, *Scientific American*, April, 1989. This study is discussed in some detail in Dr. Arthur Janov's previously referenced <u>Why You Get Sick and How You Get Well</u>, pp. 34-35.

29. <u>Paths of Life: Seven Scenarios</u> by Alice Miller, *Pantheon Books*, 1998, pp. 171-172

30. Two relevant recent articles (of many) are "Scars That Won't Heal: The Neurobiology of Child Abuse" by Martin H. Teicher, *Scientific American*, March 2002 and "Psychiatrists Explore Legacy of Traumatic Stress in Early Life" by Lynne Lamberg, *The Journal of the American Medical Association (JAMA)*, August 1, 2001, online at *http://jama.ama-assn.org/issues/v286n5/ffull/jmn0801-2.html*

31. "42 years later, those who felt loved as kids prove to be healthier" By Kate McClare, Knight-Ridder News Service, in the *San Diego Union-Tribune*, March 23, 1996.

32. Perhaps the best-known study on the topic was the Harlow experiment that subjected infant monkeys to either a "wire mother"—a form roughly shaped like an adult monkey, made of wire—or a "cloth mother," which was the same form but covered with soft cloth. Even that small bit of comfort was enough to make the babies more emotionally healthy (and better parents) than their peers who grew up with only wire-form "parents"—but of course not the same as babies raised by their actual mothers. Ashley Montagu's classic <u>Touching: The Human Significance of the Skin</u> (pp. 38-44), listed in Appendix I, "Further Reading," contains more detail on this and other research on early experience and its effects on later parenting.

33. "Breast-Feeding Mothers Less Likely to Abuse Kids," Alison McCook, *Reuters*, July 10, 2002. *http://story.news.yahoo.com/news?tmpl=story&u=/nm/20020710/hl_nm/women_children_dc_1*

34. <u>River Out of Eden: A Darwinian View of Life</u>, by Richard Dawkins, *BasicBooks*, 1995, pp. 132-133

35. "Who's in Control? The Unhappy Consequences of Being Child-Centered" by Jean Liedloff, *Mothering* magazine, Winter 1994. Posted on the web at *http://www.continuum-concept.org/reading/whosIn Control.html*

36. One good source here is the previously-referenced <u>Ghosts from the Nursery: Tracing the Roots of Violence</u>. Chapters 3 and 4 ("Before We Know It: Prenatal exposure to drugs and malnutrition" and "Love's Labor Lost: Adverse experiences in the womb and at birth") are focused on the impact of prenatal and birth events, but the entire book supports the premise of sensitivity to early conditions in humans generally.

37. An especially thorough work for a general audience is <u>Imprints: the lifelong effects of the birth experience</u> by Dr. Arthur Janov, *Coward-McCann, Inc.* 1983. From page 248:

> "In my opinion it *[a change in birth practices]* is the most important action we can take in the field of mental health. No other single factor can alter neurosis or psychosis on such a fundamental level; no diet, no conditioning, no manipulation of external circumstances, no massage, no lecture, no philosophy, no ideology, no religion, no amount of love and affection can do what a proper birth can do. . . . Ultimately, a simple change in birth practices would affect our social structure, our penal institutions, our mental hospitals and the values by which we raise our children—the next generation to inherit the Earth."

The classic <u>Birth Without Violence</u> by Frederick Leboyer is also worth mentioning here. *Healing Arts Press*, 1974, English translation 1975, *Healing Arts Press* edition 1995, or *Inner Traditions International Limited*; 2nd Revision edition 2002.

38. A few sources for information on breast-feeding: *http://webhome.idirect.com/~born2luv/PARENT.HTML*

http://www.lactations.com/home.html
http://www.compleatmother.com/
http://www.askdrsears.com/html/2/T020100.asp

<u>The Breast-feeding Book: Everything You Need to Know About Nursing Your Child from Birth Through Weaning</u> by William Sears M.D., *Little Brown and Company*, 2000
and finally (have to stop somewhere!) "Breastfeed a Toddler—Why on Earth?" at *http://www.bflrc.com/newman/breast-feeding/*

toddler. htm, which includes this:

> "... UNICEF has long encouraged breast-feeding for two years and longer, and the American Academy of Pediatrics is now on record as encouraging mothers to nurse at least one year and as long after as both mother and baby desire. Breast-feeding to 3 and 4 years of age has been common in much of the world until recently, and breast-feeding toddlers is still common in many societies."

39. Joy's article is also available on the web, at *http://www.wired.com/wired/archive/8.04/joy.html*. For balance, one of Kurzweil's websites, including some of his writing, is at *http://www.kurzweilai.net/meme/frame.html?m=10*

40. *Wired Magazine*, May 2002, p. 131

41. <u>The Biology of Love</u> by Dr. Arthur Janov, *Prometheus Books*, 2000, p. 323.

42. *http://www.washtimes.com/national/20040922-122847-5968r.htm*

43. <u>Home Schooling: From the Extreme to the Mainstream</u> by Patrick Basham, "A Frazer Institute Occasional Paper," 2001

44. The study showing that social rejection and physical pain are handled by the same region of the brain appeared in *Science*, October 2003, and was led by Naomi L. Eisenberger of the University of California at Los Angeles.

45. For instance, "The average temperature of advanced primal patients is in the low 97s."—from <u>Why You Get Sick and How You Get Well</u> by Arthur Janov, *Dove Books*, 1996, p. 224. Dr. Janov, unlike most people practicing therapy, has done, and continues to do, a great deal of physical research, often with the involvement of researchers at UCLA and elsewhere.

INDEX

Abuse:
  child, 34, 39, 88, 91, 103,
    110, 141
  spousal, 39, 95
Accretion of experience, 57
  see also Emergence
ACE Study, 110
  see also Felitti, Dr. Vincent J.
Age of Intelligent Machines, The
  (Kurzweil), 127
Ahimsa, 133
Alphabet Versus the Goddess,
  The (Shlain), 130
Attachment Parenting, 134–136
Authoritarianism, 36, 75, 122

Babies, premature, 54–55
Baby B's, 135
  see also Sears, Dr. William
Behavior:
  adult, 42, 55, 94, 130
  changes in, 16–17, 25, 41,
    123, 130
  group, 16, 79, 129
  human, 4, 9, 36, 84–85, 131
  loving, 102–103, 105, 109
  of children, 134
  violent, 33, 60, 130
Birth:
  mechanization of, 131
  traumatic, 95

Birth Without Violence
  (Leboyer), 120, 134
Black Book of Communism, The
  (Courtis et al.), 66–67
Break the cycle, 109, 124
Breast-feeding, 58, 103, 111,
  122, 135
Buddhist(s)/(ism), 4, 93, 101,
  133, 151

Capitalism, 70
Centralized:
  bureaucracy, 24
  control, 26, 64
  power, 15, 27, 41, 43, 129
  systems, 117
Change:
  happens when enough people
    share the necessary
    understanding, 30, 36, 118
  importance of, 16, 83
  in behavior, 16–17, 41, 123
  one's paradigm, 20, 25
  the world, 1, 21, 40, 43, 49,
    119, 142
Chaos Theory, 15, 56
  see also Complexity Theory
Character:
  adult, 30, 33, 42, 55
  molded by early experiences, 5,
    34, 53–54, 60
  see also Emergence

Character *(cont.)*:
  of society, 15, 45
  of the world, 16, 24, 121, 142
Charity:
  government, 73
  non-coercive, 76
Children, treatment of, 4, 16, 25,
    30–31, 37, 42, 48, 61, 80, 96,
    108, 119–121, 130–131, 134
  see also Seven Points
Christian(s)/(ity), 4, 93, 101
CICO (Compassion In,
  Compassion Out), 61
Civil Disobedience (Thoreau), 77
Coercion:
  attempts to create a better
    world via, 69
  government, 28, 68, 77, 79, 129
  initiated, 63, 66, 69, 79–80, 122
  Socialist, 70
  systematic, 10
  unfreedom, 30, 35, 117
  world with less, 43
Coercive:
  government, 67, 72, 77, 79,
    129, 140
  non-, 19, 71, 75, 139
  regulation, 70
  socialism, 69, 73, 80
  state power, 68, 78, 129
Columbus, Christopher, 46, 47
Commun(ism)/(ist), 66–70
Communist Manifesto, The
  (Marx), 66
Compassion:
  and non-violence, 133
  as a guiding force for love, 98
  at the expense of freedom, 66
  see also Marxism

combined with love and
    respect, 61, 76, 119
  environment of, 1
  for children, 108
  in politics, 80
  love and, 13, 15, 43
Compassionate:
  birth, 111
  sensitivity, 98
  world, 3, 28, 41, 43, 49, 96
Complex systems:
  exhibit sensitive dependence on
    early conditions, 15, 56, 120
  to succeed with, 26
Complexity Theory:
  applied to human beings, 15
  evolution, 56
  see also Chaos Theory
Continuum Concept (Liedloff),
  107
Control, centralized, 26–27, 40,
  64, 77
C-section, 122

Dawkins, Richard, 104
Death by Government (Rummel),
  67
Decentralized systems, 27–28
Defenses, 3, 38, 64, 83, 89, 101
Dental plaque, 55
Dependence, sensitive, 15, 34, 44,
  55, 60, 96
Disease:
  elimination of, 20
  infectious, 20–24, 26, 40, 126
Divine right of kings, 69
DNA, 25, 43, 56, 107
Dog(s), 25, 56, 101–105, 122

Dream, 9
Drugs, 3, 8–9, 16, 34, 38, 58–59,
    74–75, 88, 109, 121, 141
*Dumbing Us Down: The Hidden
    Curriculum of Compulsory
    Schooling* (Gatto), 139
Dyslexia, 138

Emergence:
    basic law of nature, 28
    defined, 25, 27
Emergent system, 25–28, 77, 117
Emerson, Ralph Waldo, 83, 125
Emotional:
    damage, 14–16, 42, 57–58, 61,
        70, 84–85, 91–94, 128–129
    defenses, 3
    health, 22, 31–32, 35, 42, 71, 76,
        101–102, 109, 115, 118–120,
        124–125, 129–131
    plague, 7, 8
    see also Human condition
Engels, Friedrich, 66, 68
Evil:
    coercive power, 78
    defined, 32
    ending, 3
    hidden nature of, 86
    human, 10, 13, 16, 30–32
Experience:
    early, 5, 15, 33–34, 36, 42,
        54–60, 94, 120, 130
    later, 34, 57, 60, 94, 130

Falun Gong, 71, 93
FDA (Food and Drug
    Administration), 74
Feeling Child, The (Janov), 96

Feelings as guideposts to
    appropriate behavior, 102, 131
Felitti, Dr. Vincent J., 91, 110
*For Your Own Good: Hidden
    Cruelty in Childhood and the
    Roots of Violence* (Miller), 75
Framework(s), structure, 1, 3, 5,
    19, 20, 24, 32, 41, 48
    see also Paradigm(s)
*Free at Last: The Sudbury Valley
    School* (Greenberg), 139
Freedom:
    at the expense of love, 65
    economic, 71
    empowered by future
        technology, 81
    enables harmony, 107
    in human affairs, 75
    necessary part of love, 30, 35,
        117
    requires love, 76
    to create prosperity, 73
    versus tyranny, 4, 35, 81, 142
Freud, Sigmund, 7

Galilei, Galileo, 47
Gandhi, 66, 77
Gatto, John Taylor, 139
Genetics, 33, 53, 128, 130
Genocide, 1, 3, 32, 38–39, 78
Gentle birth:
    as a solid foundation for a
        child, 111
    improving life, 120
    planning for, 109, 122
    trend towards, 36
    see also Leboyer
Germ Theory of Disease, 21–24,
    41, 116

GIGO (Garbage In, Garbage
   Out), 61
Glimpse of Heaven, 63
   see also Sunde, Karen
Government:
   atrocity, 118
   coercive, 38, 66–79, 129–130
   non- organizations, 75
   non- school, 139
   restrained, 73
   restricted power, 124
   school(s)/(ing), 136, 140
   torture, 124
Greenberg, Daniel, 138–139
   see also Sudbury Valley
      School
Gulag(s), 13, 70, 75
Gum disease, 55

Headquarters, Paradigm, 40
Healthy:
   loving adults, 30, 34–35, 39,
      119
   world, 30, 35
Heart, issues of the, 4
Hemispheric-dominance
   imbalance, 130
Herbert, Auberon, 65
Hindu(ism), 4, 133
Hitler, Adolph, 70, 75–76
Holt, John, 139
Home schooling, 140
Hugo, Victor, 115
Human condition, 2, 7, 15–16,
   29, 36, 38, 48, 53, 57, 60, 83,
   85, 87, 94, 109
Human evil:
   defined, 32
   no longer present, 13

world without, 10, 16
Human rights, 43, 73, 124
Human world:
   character of, 24, 142
   creating, 76
   healthier, 35, 39, 44
   is as we make it, 30
   nature of, 2, 28, 116
   transform the, 38

I, Pencil (Read), 76
Indians, American, 65
Induced births, 55
Infants, treatment of, 4, 16, 25,
   30–33, 35, 37, 42, 48, 61, 80,
   93, 95, 119–121, 124, 130–131,
   133–134
   see also Seven Points
Inner Beauty, Inner Light: Yoga
   for Pregnant Women
   (Leboyer), 134

Jain(ism), 101, 133–134
Janov, Dr. Arthur, 38, 53, 96, 97,
   101, 133, 136
Jefferson, Thomas, 77
Joy, Bill, 127–129, 131

Keaton, Diane, 84
Keneally, Thomas, 84
   see also Schindler's List
Khmer Rouge, 8, 119
Killing Fields, The, 8
King, Martin Luther, 77
King, Stephen, 89
Kramer, Dr. Michael, 54

Kuhn, Thomas, 19
  see also Paradigm(s)
Kurzweil, Ray, 127, 131

Leboyer:
  Dr. Frederick, 15, 36, 97–98,
    120, 134
  Gentle Birth, 97
Legacy, 81, 124
Lenin, Vladimir, 68
Liedloff, Jean, 107–108
Life expectancy, 21, 125
Lifetime sentence, 38
  see also Janov, Dr. Arthur
Linking treatment of the young
  with the character of the world
  at large, 16
  see also Seven Points
Lord of the Rings (Tolkien), 78
Love:
  and compassion, 1, 4, 13, 15,
    41, 43, 61, 68, 98, 116–117,
    119–120, 124, 130–131, 142
  and freedom, 30, 35–36, 43, 63–
    65, 68, 75–80, 116–117, 121,
    125, 130, 136
  and freedom logo, 81
  and respect, 34, 37, 61, 64,
    134–136, 141
    see also Seven Points
  as a powerful force, 110
  at the expense of freedom, 65
    see also Marxism
  can save the world, 13–14, 41,
    98
  compassion and respect, 119,
    121

definition, 98
early, 34, 39, 134
feeling, 35, 95–97, 101, 103
freedom and prosperity, 77
healing power of, 14
healthy benefits of, 58, 93
heart of, 98
objective definition, 99, 102, 109
prevents damage, 15, 33
subjective definition, 99
*Loving Hands: The Traditional
  Art of Baby Massage*
  (Leboyer), 134
Low birthweight babies, 54, 59

Marketplace, 74–77, 121
Marx:
  (ism), 43, 65–66, 73
  (ist), 66, 68, 70, 72–73, 79
  Karl, 66, 68
Masses, controlling the, 68–69, 80
"Meaning is feeling", 101
  see also Janov, Dr. Arthur
Meyers, Nancy, 84
Military-industrial complex, 79
Miller, Alice, 75, 94
Mindset, 20
  see also Paradigm(s)

National Institutes of Health
  (NIH), 55
Nature versus nurture, 53
Nazi, 70, 84, 119
Neill, A.S., 136–137
Neurosis, 38–39, 49, 55–56, 92,
  94, 109–110, 118, 126, 129,
  134, 136, 142
Neurotics, 131

New World, 36, 43, 47–48, 92,
    128, 142
Newborns, treatment of, 31–32,
    61
Nietzsche, Friedrich, 85
Non-violence, 133
Nuclear:
    arsenals, 75, 131
Nuclear (cont.):
    bomb, 128
    thermo-, 142
    tipped missiles, 39
    weapons, 129

Old World, 46, 141
Oligarchs, 73
On Authority (Engels), 68

Paine, Thomas, 115
Papillon, 105
Paradigm(s)/(atic):
    change, 40, 64, 142
    defined, 19, 40
    framework, 127
    how they work, 23–24, 36,
        40–41
    new, 37, 46
    power of, 20, 41, 117, 123
    President of, 40
    replacing old, 3, 25
    science as a, 20–24
    shift, 45, 64
    tools, 17, 25, 28, 116, 118
Paradise:
    better world, 2, 16, 19, 22,
        31–32, 80, 125–127, 141–142
    earthly, 115

Paradigm, 29–30, 36, 41, 45,
    49, 109, 115–117, 123–124
Penalties for being productive,
    72, 80
Perceptions of reality, 3
    see also Paradigm(s)
Perceptual shift(s), 3, 64
    see also Paradigm shift
Perfection, 22, 31, 41, 43
Points, Seven, 30
    see also Paradise Paradigm
Pol Pot, 7, 43
Police state, 16, 43, 119, 121, 142
Polio:
    disease, 20–21
    vaccine, 40
    see also Salk, Dr. Jonas
Power:
    as an abuse, 70
    centralized, 15, 27, 43
    coercive, 67, 72, 78–79, 130
    elite, 73, 80
    government, 69–70, 78, 124
    of early experience, 56, 60, 94
    of emergence, 25, 28, 118
    of freedom, 73
    of intellectual knowledge, 94
    of paradigms, 20, 25, 41,
        116–117, 123
    state, 78, 129
Prediction, 3, 126–127
Predisposition, genetic, 130
Preferences, 4, 64
Pregnant Mothers/Women,
    treatment of, 25, 31, 35, 42, 55,
        59–60, 119–121, 131
    see also Seven Points
Premature babies, 54–55
Prevention, 57, 89, 91–92
Prince The Wonder Dog, 106

Prosperity, 1, 64, 71–73, 77–79
Prostaglandin, 55
Psychological defenses, 64
Psychopathology, 7, 10, 39

Raising enough emotionally
  healthy children will create a
  healthy world, 31, 36, 116, 120,
  124
  see also Paradise Paradigm
Rape, 42, 48, 65, 130
Read, Leonard E., 76
Real Self, 85, 88
Red Cross, 73–74
Rees, Martin, 128–129, 131
Regulation:
  coercive, 70, 74
  government, 73
  market, 74
  of behavior, 102
Reich, Wilhelm, 7, 8
Religion(s), 1, 3–4, 71, 94, 101,
  116
Reward for non-productivity, 72,
  80
Rummel, Professor R.J., 67

'Salem's Lot (King), 89
Salk, Dr. Jonas, 40
Salvation Army, 75
Save the world, 13–14, 36–37, 41,
  48, 89, 98
  see also Paradise Paradigm
Schindler's List (Keneally), 84
Schopenhauer, Arthur, 133
Schooling:
  government, 136
  home, 140

typical, 138
Un- movement, 139
Science, paradigm of, 20–21
Sears, Dr. William & Mrs.
  Martha, 135
Self-esteem, 95
Sensitive dependence on early
  conditions, 15, 34, 96
  see also Complex Systems
Sentient machines, 132
Seven Points, 30
  see also Paradise Paradigm
Shaw, George Bernard, 80
Shlain, Dr. Leonard, 130
Slavery, 63, 65
Sleeper, 93
Smallpox, 20–21
Smoking:
  and pregnant mothers, 59
  as a drug, 34, 109
  effects on fetus, 58–59
Social(ism)/(ist), 68–73, 80
Sociopath(ic), 33, 42, 70–72, 93,
  131
Something's Gotta Give, 84, 85
Spencer, Herbert, 65, 79
Spielberg, Steven, 84
Stalin, Joseph, 67
Star Wars Episode III, 77
Strathearn, Dr. Lane, 54, 103
Stress, 23, 53, 59, 141
Structure of Scientific
  Revolutions, The (Kuhn), 19
Sudbury Valley School, 108,
  136, 138–139
Summerhill School, 108, 136–139
Summerhill: A Radical Approach
  To Child Rearing (Neill), 136
Sunde, Karen, 63

Teicher, Martin H., 91
The child is father to the man,
15, 33, 60
Thoreau, Henry David, 63, 77, 97
Tolkien, J.R.R., 77–78
Totalitarianism, 119
Transformation, Paradise, 38
see also Paradise Paradigm
Trauma(tic):
early, 55–57, 60, 89, 93, 95
event, 84
later, 109, 120
repression of, 95, 102, 109, 118
126
Treatment of the young, 16, 24,
31, 35–37, 61, 116, 120, 122
Tyranny, 3–4, 35, 61, 68, 78, 81,
84, 122, 127, 134, 142

Underwriters Laboratories (UL),
73, 74
Unfreedom, 35, 117
Unschooling movement, 139
Utopia, 2, 68, 70

Vampires, 87–89
Violence, 30, 33, 41, 49, 57, 60,
65–66, 68–69, 84, 89, 91, 94,
130, 141
Virus, computer, 128–129
Vitamin and supplement
industry, 74
Voluntary:
cooperation, 76
group, 71
system, 77
Voluntaryism, A Plea For
(Herbert), 65

Wealth:
creation of, 71
erosion of, 69, 72
forced transfer of, 69
material, 126
production of, 80
Welfare, corporate, 79
Werewolves, 86–87
Why the Future Doesn't Need Us
(Joy), 127
Wired Magazine, 127
Women, standing of in a society,
20–21, 130
Workshop, weekend, 95
World:
compassionate, 3, 13, 28, 41,
43, 49, 68–69, 96
healthy, 4, 25, 29, 30–32, 35–36,
42, 49, 71, 77, 115–120, 127,
129
human, 2, 30, 38–39, 44, 61,
76, 116, 142
loving, 49, 118
of your heart, 1, 81
War I, 67
War II, 67
without evil, 10, 31

Yequana Tribe, 107–108
Yin and Yang, 63